What people are saying about …

THE BLACKSMITH'S DISCIPLINE

"I have led men for fifty-one years. I am continually amazed at how many men lack spiritual depth and find themselves living in the misty lowlands of mediocrity. All men long for a cause to die for, a challenge to embrace, and loved ones to protect. The problem is, few men know how to get there. Vince presents a compelling argument for living a godly life and how to cultivate a meaningful existence that honors the Lord. Unwrapping the Scripture with exceptional clarity, citing supporting examples, providing thought-provoking questions for reflection, and offering helpful suggestions leading to spiritual maturity will help you become a man after God's heart."

Greg Bourgond, DMin, EdD, adjunct professor at University of
Northwestern and president and founder of Heart of a Warrior Ministries

"Vince Miller models his Resolute ministry to men with transparency, openness, honesty, and vulnerability. These are the keys to discipling and building godly men—and when we build godly men, everyone wins!"

Brian Doyle, president and founder of Iron Sharpens Iron

"Vince is living Hebrews 10:24 as he embodies what it means to spur one another on toward love and good deeds and to be ALL IN and bring God glory by living out our faith authentically and boldly! Vince's special sauce is his ability to hit right at the heart of challenges men face and drive our response as warriors in the fight as Christ followers and kingdom builders. I am a better man for knowing Vince and thank God for his genuine and Spirit-led focus on seeing men live to the fullest that God intended for us on this short time we have here on earth. Live All In!"

John Young, US Army veteran and leader of small groups in
multiple churches across the US for over twenty years

FORGED

GODLY MEN

THE
BLACKSMITH'S
DISCIPLINE

—

HONING
GODLY MEN

DAVID C COOK®

transforming lives together

THE BLACKSMITH'S DISCIPLINE
Published by David C Cook
4050 Lee Vance Drive
Colorado Springs, CO 80918 U.S.A.

Integrity Music Limited, a Division of David C Cook
Brighton, East Sussex BN1 2RE, England

DAVID C COOK®, the graphic circle C logo and related marks are registered trademarks of David C Cook.

Library of Congress Control Number 2024949412
ISBN 978-0-8307-8715-9
eISBN 978-0-8307-8716-6

The Team: Luke McKinnon, Jeff Gerke, James Hershberger, Brian Mellema, Jack Campbell, Karen Sherry
Cover Design: Micah Kandros

Printed in the United States of America
First Edition 2025

1 2 3 4 5 6 7 8 9 10

121824

To my first grandchild, Everett William Engen. You were thrust suddenly into this world, and the first few months were challenging. You struggled and fought, little warrior. May God bless you in your journey of growth, and may God forge you with great discipline for his glory.

CHAPTERS

To view an introductory video to this study, please visit https://beresolute.org/forged/.

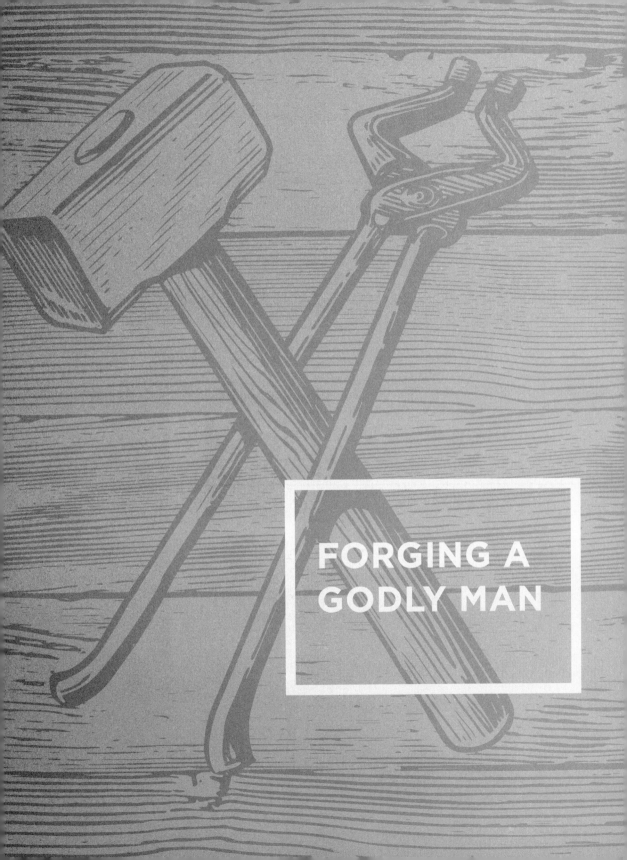

FORGING A
GODLY MAN

Men are like raw metal waiting to be forged by the hands of the Master Blacksmith, Jesus.

Every man must be forged, but only the Master Blacksmith can forge him.

His vision and discipline transform a man's molten ore into a unique and intricate object. He fashions, forms, folds, and forges all the raw elements. With discipline, he shapes a raw man into something useful and purposeful.

But a man must submit to the Blacksmith's tools as they mold his motive, intent, and desire for divine use. With the rhythmic clang of the hammer on an anvil, his discipline forges our spiritual discipline, strengthening our character and shaping us for his unique use.

It can be an unpleasant and fiery process.

The Blacksmith must stoke the flames to temper the metal (and the mettle) of a man. A man of God must be heated in the fires of faith. In the fire, he is heated, purified, and softened. Then with each strike of the Blacksmith's hammer, his spiritual faculties are formed, shaping his discernment and fortifying his resolve to prepare him for the trials of life. Submission is required to reveal a man's calling. He must subject himself to the vision, tools, and discomfort of the Blacksmith's discipline.

The Master Blacksmith's discipline reveals a godly man when (and because) he submits to it. Spiritual discipline is forged into him. The byproducts are heightened spiritual awareness, sharpened character, and ever-increasing glory to God displayed through his ministry.

Submission is required to reveal a man's calling.

In a world fraught with careless, conflicted, and confused men, a disciplined and godly man is a forged work of courage and clarity. His life is a testament to Jesus, the Master Blacksmith.

THE TOOLS OF THE BLACKSMITH

In this book, we will explore five essential spiritual disciplines that serve as the hammer, tongs, chisel, files, and brushes on the anvil of spiritual growth. Each tool strikes upon the behavior and intent of a man's soul, forging him according to God's vision.

The disciplines are not optional; they are essential. They mold and shape us as men. They must be both forged in us and wielded by us, as they aid in the process of becoming the men God designed us to be. These timeless tools have been handed down for generations and were the same tools Jesus used with his men. Followers have since passed these down from one man to another. They are beneficial regardless of our physical age or spiritual stage and useful for both the novice in faith and the mature. These disciplines are relevant today just as they were to men two thousand years ago.

However, they are not the means of our salvation.

The five disciplines in this book are merely tools. They fire spiritual growth, but they do not forge our salvation. As we swing the hammer of each discipline, we must remember that it was Jesus who forged our salvation. Jesus is the one who rescues us from sin, which separates us from God. Our salvation is secured and complete through his life, death, and resurrection. The tools we will wield are only a means of connection and growth that result from his work.

Though they are tools and nothing more, they are critical tools that we should wield regularly. They are crucial in our training, and they shape how a man lives a godly life. Here is how one older mentor said it to his younger disciple:

Train yourself for godliness. (1 Tim. 4:7)

Within this book are the divine tools that train us as God's disciples and direct us to his godliness.

REFLECTION AND DISCUSSION QUESTIONS

1. Reflect on the analogy of men being like molten metal waiting to be forged by Jesus, the Master Blacksmith. How does this imagery resonate with your understanding of personal growth and transformation in your spiritual journey?

2. Discuss the significance of the spiritual disciplines as tools for shaping men into the image that God designed them to be. If you've used one or more of these before, which discipline has had the most impact on your life, and why?

FORGED BY THE BLACKSMITH

Before we begin, let's look at a story told by the Master Blacksmith to learn why the tools are necessary:

> "Everyone then who hears these words of mine and does them will be like a wise man who built his house on the rock. And the rain fell, and the floods came, and the winds blew and beat on that house, but it did not fall, because it had been founded on the rock. And everyone who hears these words of mine and does not do them will be like a foolish man who built his house on the sand. And the rain fell, and the floods came, and the winds blew and beat against that house, and it fell, and great was the fall of it."
>
> And when Jesus finished these sayings, the crowds were astonished at his teaching. (Matt. 7:24–28)

In these words, Jesus offers profound and simple wisdom. He describes two distinct men: one foolish and one wise. Each man is constructing his own life, his visible and readily seen life. However, the critical disparity lies in the foundations upon which their lives are built—one on sand, the other on rock. While both structures look similar at first glance, they are not. Onlookers may miss it, but the disparity is in the unseen foundation. The foundations, while unseen, are radically different. The foolish man's life is built on the shifting sand of his own principles and desires, while the wise man's life is built on the steadfast rock of submission to the principles and desires of Jesus Christ.

Then enters the great drama: a terrific storm.

Both men are tested by it. The storm exposes the integrity of each man's life. What it was built upon and where it was built were radically different in each case. The storm reveals the unseen integrity—or lack thereof.

Jesus's point is that every man will encounter a storm. The storm will test the integrity of how and where each man has built his life. It will expose him regardless of how good he may look on the outside. But what it will ultimately expose is what he has built his life upon—his own principles and desires or the Master Blacksmith's principles and desires.

Life's storms expose all men. The storms you face will expose your unseen integrity. This is an epic test for all of us. It should immediately prompt us to consider vital questions such as these:

> Is my life nothing but show?
> What have I built my life upon?
> Am I ready for the inevitable storm?

Some men spend their entire lives pretending, believing they have everyone fooled. But Jesus says they are fools. False integrity might work for a while, but ultimately, it's a smoke screen that sets us up for a catastrophic fall.

Right now, you might feel like the veneer of your life is presentable and properly under control, but are there any vulnerabilities? The storm will come; it's inevitable. When it does, it will test you, revealing your true integrity and exposing the foundation of your life, which divides men—the foolish from the wise. Can you confidently declare you are prepared and ready?

Instead of waiting, why not prepare? Why not begin right now cultivating a life of integrity, building on a solid foundation, and fortifying yourself against the next storm?

The place to prepare is in the Blacksmith's forge, where men are molded by his discipline.

SPIRITUAL DISCIPLINES ARE THE TOOLS

To begin, we need a few tools. We don't need many, though. Five are enough. They are not fancy or full of features. They're simple and straightforward, and they get the job done. Any man can become proficient at using them. Just as the blacksmith requires a simple selection of tools—hammer, tongs, chisel, files, and brushes—we will focus on five effective tools for men that we can grasp and use with great efficiency.

In the coming chapters, we will learn how to master the tools that help us integrate the Master's teachings. The goal is to make these tools uncomplicated and understandable for men of any age. If you are a young man, you will be able to draw from these disciplines for the rest of your life. If you are older and have experience with the disciplines, you might consider how to use them at new levels of competency or even train others to use them. Regardless, they are the five for forging integrity in men.

The tools will inform and produce results in two aspects of our lives: the private and the public. The first two tools, prayer and Scripture, frequently begin as private disciplines but must mature into public expression. The following three—brotherhood, accountability, and ministry—are the catalysts for our private discipline and move us into public view. Faithful engagement with these tools is how men are spiritually forged so we build our lives on the Master Blacksmith's teaching and foundation.

Here is an outline of the next five chapters and tools.

> **Through prayer, a man surrenders his will to God and experiences transformative power.**

ONE | THE TOOL OF PRAYER

Speaking with our unseen God.

Prayer is a fundamental spiritual discipline. It is an intimate conversation between a man and God in which he can express his deepest thoughts, desires, and concerns. Prayer is a tool for forging intimacy with God, submitting our will, and finding contentment in the fires of life. Through prayer, a man surrenders his will to God and experiences the transformative power of divine connection to the source of all life.

TWO | THE TOOL OF SCRIPTURE

Hearing from God by reading his Word.

Men desire the truth and are on a quest to discover it. Scripture reveals all truth, and Jesus embodies it. Without Scripture, we cannot know the truth. It is essential for a man's spiritual growth to read Scripture and be renewed by it. It serves as a guide for navigating life's challenges and finding a direction in line with God's teachings. By subjecting to the tool and wielding it as a weapon, a man gains wisdom, direction, and correction, enabling him to live a life that integrates with God's will.

THREE | THE TOOL OF BROTHERHOOD

Sharpening our lives with spiritual brothers.

Many men struggle to form meaningful connections with other men, and the few relationships they do have often lack spiritual depth. As a result, men may choose to navigate life alone, missing out on the opportunity to connect with others as fellow believers. However, men who understand the value of brotherhood know that the experience of sharpening one another is essential for personal growth and development. Having brothers is necessary to help us become better men.

FOUR | THE TOOL OF ACCOUNTABILITY

Submitting willingly to accountability.

Accountability is frequently misunderstood and misused in spiritual brotherhood. Accountability is shrouded in misconception, eliciting apprehensions in men that conjure up ideas of strange and rigid rituals. However, accountability can be a positive and proactive discipline. If we learn a new approach, accountability will become a useful tool for forging positive and lasting change.

FIVE | THE TOOL OF MINISTRY

Doing ministry through active obedience.

Christian men who are accelerating their spiritual growth are involved in some form of ministry that aligns with their gifts and talents. Transitioning from experiencing ministry to actively doing ministry can be a powerful awakening for men. Men who are actively engaged in the tool of ministry find unique ways to use their gifts, passions, and talents for the kingdom's benefit. It may sound challenging, but it is an exhilarating experience in the forge.

> **Men who are actively engaged in the tool of ministry find unique ways to use their gifts, passions, and talents for the kingdom's benefit.**

Forging these five disciplines into the essential elements of our lives will strengthen our resolve and refine our mettle, but this requires our active engagement. As we embrace these simple, self-imposed disciplines, we are refined. They are tools for forging a dynamic relationship with God.

With that, let's step into the workshop and submit to the Master Blacksmith's discipline.

REFLECTION AND DISCUSSION QUESTIONS

1. Reflect on the parable of the wise and foolish builders as told by Jesus. How does this story challenge you to evaluate the foundation upon which you've built your life? What steps can you take to ensure that your foundation is rooted in obedience to God's Word?

2. How can the spiritual discipline of accountability help you build a solid foundation in your faith and withstand the storms of life? Discuss any experiences you've had with positive or negative forms of accountability in your spiritual journey.

THE TOOL
OF PRAYER

There is no activity more vital in a man's life than the time forged with God in prayer.

Every activity in this life has basic, fundamental practices that lead to certain success. Tony Dungy will tell you there are fundamentals in the sport of football. Chip Gaines will tell you there are fundamentals in the work of home remodeling. John Maxwell will tell you there are fundamentals in the art and skill of leadership. In the same way, there are fundamental disciplines for the man who wants to grow in his relationship with God.

Prayer is the first of these.

Prayer must be forged faithfully into the structure of a man's life, done daily, and practiced consciously until it becomes as involuntary as breathing itself. A man of God cannot get by without prayer.

Pew Research reports that about 55 percent of Americans pray every day.[1] But this percentage sounds extraordinarily high to me. Most believing men I talk to have admitted to going long periods—days, weeks, or even months—without praying. Until we get honest about our prayer life, it's going to be hard to get to the bottom of the core issue that men have with prayer.

So, if men are not actually praying, why aren't we?

It can't be because of a lack of information or resources on how to do it. There are many resources on prayer, including sermons, books, tools, and methods covering just about every facet of prayer. In addition, dozens of popular apps incite prayer, remind you to pray, and even pray for you.

This information is helpful and insightful, and I hope you'll search out some of these resources. But if the wealth of information on the market solved the challenge of giving us robust prayer lives, there would be a majority of men presently praying ... and there is not.

> **A man of God cannot get by without prayer.**

One of the problems men have is how they think about prayer. They approach it like they approach a diet. Like the latest weight-loss fad, the results are short-lived. Dieting (usually capitalizing on the shame of excessive weight) that focuses on results in a short time is nearly always short-lived, primarily because the goal is short-lived. That is the design of a diet. They are short-term eating changes that cannot solve long-term eating problems.

What men fail to remember once they get sucked in is that they must eat for the rest of their lives. A short-term diet aimed at a long-term problem is a waste of time. Yet men still fall for the latest intermittent fasting trend or a low-carb diet that boasts fast results.

When it comes to prayer, a man doesn't need a lot of information about it or an introduction to the latest prayer trends that come and go quickly. What he needs is a new prayer lifestyle. One that is uncomplicated and easy to sustain for the rest of his life.

Prayer is a simple discipline when you think about it. It is merely having a conversation with God. Too often, excessive information about prayer deters us from grasping the basic elements of prayer. Notice that even Jesus's first followers had this same question:

> Jesus was praying in a certain place, and when he finished, one of his disciples said to him, "Lord, teach us to pray, as John taught his disciples." (Luke 11:1)

The disciples were eager to learn from the Master Blacksmith, maybe because they had never seen anybody pray like he did. They saw Jesus praying "in the forge." They were intrigued by what they saw and then implored him to teach them how to wield the tool of prayer.

Therefore, Jesus taught them how to pray using what became one of the most familiar prayers of all time: the Lord's Prayer. If you come from a liturgical tradition, you know it well.

Although Jesus was willing to provide an outline for prayer, I don't think he intended this to be the only prayer we should ever pray. In fact, the whole eleventh chapter of Luke is filled with basic teachings about prayer, which the Master Blacksmith made simple. The men wanted to do it, so he showed them how. If his teaching in Luke 11 were reduced to a single sentence, it could be: "Talk to God at any time and ask him anything."

Read for yourself:

> I tell you, ask, and it will be given to you; seek, and you will find; knock, and it will be opened to you. For everyone who asks receives, and the one who seeks finds, and to the one who knocks it will be opened. What father among you, if his son asks for a fish, will instead of a fish give him a serpent; or if he asks for an egg, will give him a scorpion? If you then, who are evil, know how to give good gifts to your children, how much more will the heavenly Father give the Holy Spirit to those who ask him! (Luke 11:9-13)

The Master provides a simple answer. He clarifies that prayer should be uncomplicated and not confined to a specific script. He uses what we have come to call the Lord's Prayer as an example for them to start with and encourages them to communicate with God freely, asking for anything, anywhere, and at any time.

That's what we are going for here. We will step into the forge and wield the tool of prayer. I will break prayer down into simple principles that will get you started in developing a new lifestyle of prayer. But first, we must address two preliminary matters: making the time and what to talk about when we pray.

REFLECTION AND DISCUSSION QUESTIONS

1. Reflect on the statement "Prayer is straightforward when you think about it. At its most basic level, it is merely having a conversation with God." How does this perspective challenge or confirm your understanding of prayer? Share any personal experiences or insights into how viewing prayer as a simple conversation with God has impacted your prayer life.

2. Consider the disciples' request to Jesus to teach them how to pray, as recorded in Luke 11:1. Why do you think they asked this question, and what can we learn from Jesus's response? Discuss how we can apply Jesus's teachings on prayer—particularly the idea of asking, seeking, and knocking—to our own prayer lives today.

MAKING THE TIME

Ten minutes spent in the presence of Christ every day, aye, two minutes, will make the whole day different. (Henry Drummond)

The main issue with prayer is making and then taking the time to pray. Most men don't do it. It's simply not on their schedules. But if it were, as Drummond said, our day would look a whole lot different.

If you want a more fulfilling spiritual life, prayer is an imperative tool. But the first step is not getting motivated, being inspired, or even expressing your intent to change. It's adding prayer to your calendar and then showing up for the scheduled time and praying.

The Master Blacksmith modeled this in Luke 11. He set a meeting with God and then he woke up, showed up, and spoke with God.

How simple is that?

This is how men learn how to wield the tool of prayer. It's not by watching another sermon about prayer, listening to an inspiring story about the power of prayer, or even reading a book (like this one) about prayer. You will learn far more about prayer and even how to do it if you just schedule a meeting with the Lord, wake up, show up, and speak up.

Think about what's more effective for learning how to forge: watching a television show about how to use a forge, or actually going to a forge and sweating in the heat, swinging the tools, grinding the iron, making mistakes, and repeating the process?

The same is true with prayer. By actually praying, we will learn more than we ever could just by watching, hearing, or reading about it. Prayer is a tool, but even

> If you want a more fulfilling spiritual life, prayer is an imperative tool.

more it's an experience with our divine God. In prayer a man's desires are laid bare on the anvil before the Master Blacksmith who forged him.

The main obstacle to prayer is not a lack of information—it's all the other pressing issues that prevent us from getting to the meeting. If we're not protective of the time, those issues will keep us from developing a productive pattern of prayer. Daily, every man faces competing demands that contend for this time. Because of this, some men endure long periods devoid of prayer, relying on human effort rather than trusting in God through prayer. The obvious reason is that all the other events made it into our schedules, and we showed up for them.

This is why so many men feel physically exhausted and spiritually depleted. They have focused all their effort and faith in their own strength, filling their calendars with meetings that have taken priority over meeting with God, who should be their top priority.

So, let's get practical.

Prayer begins with setting a time and location. This might seem rudimentary, but it's not. It's the first real step to changing your prayer pattern and experiencing the change that will come with it. Motivation is not a step, inspiration is not a step, and conviction is not a step. Determining a time and location and then showing up and doing it—now that's a step.

To get in shape, you need to take certain steps. First, you should purchase a gym membership. Second, you must set a schedule and go to the gym. Third, you need to put in the effort once you are there. If you take only the first step and simply buy a gym membership, you'll be among the 67 percent of people who pay monthly fees but never use their memberships and, as a result, never get in shape.[2]

In the same way, having membership at a church, listening to other people teach you how to pray, but never praying yourself is not going to help. What helps is actually setting a time to pray with God and showing up to that time and praying.

Progress starts with setting a specific time and location. This will establish a routine that will encourage discipline. Initially, it may feel a bit forced, but it's necessary because having a daily meeting like this over a lifetime will change not only how you pray but also your prayer habits. Consider this: If the 67 percent of people who pay for a gym membership and don't go would simply schedule and attend workouts at the gym they've already paid for, think about the positive change it would have in their lives.

FIRST | SET YOUR TIME

I suggest beginning with a five-to-ten-minute daily appointment at the same time.

Many men may feel that this is too short, but it's not. The duration, especially at the beginning, doesn't matter. What we need to do is establish a consistent routine. A prayer lifestyle isn't formed in a single lengthy session but in a repetitive pattern that we commit to for a lifetime. I've seen too many men take on more than they can handle in terms of duration and then struggle with consistency when they can't sustain it. With prayer, men should start with a short duration, do it daily, and develop a steady pattern.

Just look at what Jesus did:

> Rising very early in the morning, while it was still dark, he departed and went out to a desolate place, and there he prayed. And Simon and those who were with him searched for him, and they found him and said to him, "Everyone is looking for you." (Mark 1:35–37)

Did you see it?

He rose so early that it was still dark. He departed, he went, and he prayed.

This was common for Jesus. He was busy too—just like you. And be honest, he was far busier and more popular than you and me. There were plenty of issues, meetings, and demands upon him, and yet prayer was still on the schedule.

A prayer lifestyle isn't formed in a single lengthy session but in a repetitive pattern.

Jesus's duration was probably longer than five to ten minutes, but don't be concerned about that right now. No matter how long you work at it, your discipline will never match the Master's. But you will sometimes get lost in prayer and spend extended time with the Father. Enjoy those moments when they happen, but remember that it's the pattern we are trying to establish and maintain.

Let me be more specific about what I am asking you to do.

Put a recurring five-to-ten-minute early-morning appointment on your calendar and have it repeat daily and indefinitely. Turn on the alert as well. I like using my work calendar because I have to look at it daily. When I miss a scheduled time with God, I will be forced to stare at it for the rest of the day.

SECOND | SET YOUR LOCATION

So, now that you have set a time, you need to set a location.

> Rising very early in the morning, while it was still dark, he departed and went out to a desolate place, and there he prayed. And Simon and those who were with him searched for him, and they found him and said to him, "Everyone is looking for you." (Mark 1:35-37)

Did you see his location?

Jesus got up, left the comfort of the home, or camp, and went off to "a desolate place." Some translations say "a solitary place."

His time was early, and his location was private. He left the company of other people to be in the company of God.

That's what I want you to do. Pick a familiar and quiet location. It could be in the corner of a closet or in the confines of your car. But it needs to be a place where you will not be interrupted for five to ten minutes. Then, when prompted by your calendar, go there. Literally, stand up and take your body to this location. This will become a place that you will associate with the activity of prayer, and soon, just being there will help you pray.

We are trying to build a psychological association with the place you go to pray. It is like the association we make with a gym where we exercise, a dining table where we eat, a bed where we sleep, or an office where we work.

Building a prayer pattern requires our attention and focus. There are many distractions in life, including people, devices, pressures, and issues. These things may be important, but they cannot follow us into our location of prayer. We must get up and leave them behind, like Jesus did.

I have learned that there are certain activities that require all of me. For example, when I go to the theater, I need to turn my phone off. When I go to bed, I need to turn the lights off. When I am having dinner with my family, I need to turn the television off. I do this because I know the activity or the person requires all of me. The same is true with prayer. We need all of

God and he wants all of us. Setting a location that is free of distractions allows me to give all my attention only to him for a few moments.

Establish a location that is all your own, where you and God can interact without interruption. There are lots of places that could work for you: a quiet office, an outdoor trail, the back porch of your home, or even a quiet car ride on the way to work. But it needs to be a silent place with few distractions so you can talk with God without interruption.

Are you ready to set your time and location for daily prayer with God?

REFLECTION AND DISCUSSION QUESTIONS

1. Reflect on the statement "The main issue with prayer is making and then taking the time to pray." Why do you think many men struggle to prioritize prayer in their daily lives? Share any personal experiences or challenges you've faced in making time for prayer.

2. Consider the practical steps outlined for making time for prayer, such as setting a specific time and location. How do you think these can help establish a consistent pattern of prayer? Discuss any strategies or techniques you've found effective in making time for prayer amidst a busy schedule.

MAKING A PACT

True prayer is measured by weight, not by length. A single groan
before God may have more fullness of prayer in it than a fine oration
of great length. (Charles Spurgeon)

Next, we need to know what to discuss when we arrive at our meeting time and location. In other words, is there a right way to structure our conversation with God?

Men often hesitate to ask this question. We may even feel embarrassed about our ignorance on the matter. Prayer can seem mysterious because we communicate with someone we have never seen. At first it feels like we are merely talking to ourselves, which raises some valid questions:

> What do I say to God?
> Are there things I shouldn't say?
> Can I be mad when I talk to God?
> Who do I pray to: God, Jesus, or the Spirit?
> Are certain topics off-limits?
> How do I start and finish a prayer?
> What if I forget to say something?
> Is there a correct posture for prayer?
> Do I need to close my eyes?
> What if I have nothing to say or run out of things
> to talk about?

These are all great questions. Over the years, I have asked all of these myself. But we can resolve each of them and learn how to pray with a simple acrostic: PACT. We will use this acrostic to structure our prayer times and address these important questions.

PACT stands for:

> » **P**ray aloud
> » **A**sk
> » **C**onfess
> » **T**hank

FIRST | PRAY ALOUD

Going a little farther, [Jesus] fell with his face to the ground and prayed, "My Father, if it is possible, may this cup be taken from me. Yet not as I will, but as you will." (Matt. 26:39 NIV)

There are so many interesting details in every one of Jesus's prayers. But did you notice the sensory detail that Matthew captured in Jesus's prayer quoted above? Matthew wrote about what Jesus was praying, which means that *Matthew could hear Jesus praying.* It seems that Jesus prayed out loud, perhaps most of the time, if not all the time.

You should do the same. When you arrive at your meeting time and location, simply begin conversing out loud with God as you would with anyone else.

I recognize that many men pray in their minds, and there is nothing wrong with this, but sometimes it's not helpful for eliminating the distractions stirring around in their heads. I believe many men fail to pray with any level of effectiveness because they cannot stay focused on prayer with God when they pray only in their minds.

Just think, if Jesus had prayed only in his head, how many moments would we have missed in the Gospels? The prayer following his baptism that launched his ministry, the prayer on the Mount of Transfiguration, the prayer at the feeding of the five thousand, and the prayer at Lazarus's tomb, among others, are significant events. Thankfully, Jesus was willing to model prayer by praying out loud. His spoken prayers exemplify what prayer should be. He never prayed aloud for show, but he understood that an abstract activity like prayer is best learned by listening to others. So, he allowed his men to listen in.

When I pray, I have found that praying aloud helps me stay focused. I am required to turn thoughts and musings into complete sentences and spoken confessions, which results in a longer and more focused time of communication with God. It even helps to hear myself saying the words. I simply imagine the Father before me and speak aloud as if he is right there with me.

It might take some getting used to, and my wife and kids have accidentally overheard me a few times. But they are better for it, just like the disciples were when they caught Jesus praying.

Jesus was not the only one to pray out loud in the Bible. Listen to how one of the ancients spoke with God.

> The LORD used to speak to Moses face to face, as a man speaks to his friend. (Ex. 33:11)

This exemplifies the type of relationship God desires to have with all people. It's exactly what Jesus demonstrated. It's also the kind of connection God wants to have with you: a genuine conversational relationship.

Do this: This week, go to your time and location and pray aloud for five to ten minutes each day.

Pro tip: Place an empty chair before you, imagine Jesus there, and then talk to him.

Praying aloud is the P in our PACT acrostic.

SECOND | ASK

> Ask, and it will be given to you; seek, and you will find; knock, and it will be opened to you. (Matt. 7:7)

I have the impression that Jesus is challenging us to ask. This is the essence of prayer, the tool we use for asking, seeking, and knocking. In prayer, we are encouraged to bring all our concerns to God without overthinking. We should be confident in his willingness to listen to us.

Prayer is not about grammatical perfection or meticulous articulation but about opening our hearts and mouths to God and making our requests known to him. Prayer is the active engagement of your desires with the desires of the Father. As we open our mouths and ask things of him and from him, we will discover more about him and ourselves. In persistence, we learn how to ask and what to ask for, discovering his blessings, favor, and perfect plan. But we need to stop worrying about what to ask and just ask.

> **We need to stop worrying about what to ask and just ask.**

Go ahead—ask him.

When you ask, pay attention. Over time, you'll begin to see the connection between your requests and his responses. He will always give the best answer for you, even if it's not the answer you expect. Your Father has your best in mind, even if it does not exactly match what you have in mind. Sometimes, he will answer immediately; other times, not so much. Sometimes, as you anticipate his answer, he will show you a better question with a totally different answer. God will respond in many unique and interesting ways that will teach you how to ask and will draw you into a deep understanding of who he is and what he wants to do in you.

But all this happens only when we dare to ask.

Do this: Ask God for one thing and persist with it, paying attention to what God does in you and with your request over many days.

Pro tip: Keep a list of these requests in a prayer journal and add dates to them.

THIRD | CONFESS

Therefore, confess your sins to one another and pray for one another, that you may be healed. The prayer of a righteous person has great power as it is working. (James 5:16)

Next in our acrostic is confession.

The term *confession* may not be commonly used today, but its meaning is relatively simple. It signifies admission, acknowledgment, or agreement with God, particularly in reference to our sins.[3] When we confess to God something we have done in disobedience to him, we agree with him about what he already knows about us. Through confession, we become increasingly transparent with him, showing that we are aware of our actions and are willing to change.

> **We don't need to pretend with God like we tend to do with people.**

The most authentic and transparent relationship we can have is with God. We don't need to pretend with God like we tend to do with people. He already knows everything, so there is no reason to hide or fake anything in prayer.

We talk to him about things he already knows, not because he doesn't know, but to confess that we know. Confession cleanses the soul and realigns our spirit with his Spirit. However, men typically avoid this because they prefer pretending, hiding, concealing, and deflecting over confession.

In Genesis 3, God gives Adam an opportunity to confess. But notice how Adam responds:

They heard the sound of the LORD God walking in the garden in the cool of the day, and the man and his wife hid themselves from the presence of the LORD God among the trees of the garden. But the LORD God called to the man and said to him, "Where are you?" And he said, "I heard the sound of you in the garden, and I was afraid, because I was naked, and I hid myself." He said, "Who told you that you were naked? Have you eaten of the tree of which I commanded you not to eat?" The man said, "The woman whom you gave to be with me, she gave me fruit of the tree, and I ate." (Gen. 3:8–12)

Adam's response is laughable. Instead of openly confessing his disobedience and lack of leadership, of which God was entirely aware, Adam blames "the woman whom you [God] gave." This is not only cowardly but is also a backhanded way of blaming God rather than just confessing his failure. God was daring him to confess, but instead, Adam blamed and hid, representing how some men behave in their relationships with God.

This response is sheer stupidity. There is no need to hide from God when we pray. He knows everything. If we choose to blame or hide, we will only embarrass ourselves in what should be the most freeing conversation we will ever have.

The best talks I've ever had with God have been moments of open confession. These are prayers of emotion and abandonment. They are the most freeing and daring conversations a man will ever have.

Listen to this confession by King David after he was openly busted by God for his adultery with Bathsheba:

Purge me with hyssop, and I shall be clean;
　　wash me, and I shall be whiter than snow.
Let me hear joy and gladness;
　　let the bones that you have broken rejoice.
Hide your face from my sins,
　　and blot out all my iniquities.
Create in me a clean heart, O God,
　　and renew a right spirit within me.
Cast me not away from your presence,
　　and take not your Holy Spirit from me.
Restore to me the joy of your salvation,
　　and uphold me with a willing spirit. (Ps. 51:7–12)

Each time I read David's confession, I am reminded of three things. First, I believe he cried this confession out loud to God. Second, it became a song that was sung publicly. Third, the confessing man is the most courageous man alive. He is the man after God's own heart. He is never proud of his sin, but he is proud of his God and is willing to let his problems, pride, and petition become his praise. And we should aspire to have the same courage David had to willingly look at our sin and sinful desires and confess them to the God of the universe, who already knows but wants us to know that we know we are sinful men who desire the joy of his salvation.

> **The confessing man is the most courageous man alive.**

So, are you ready to make your confession? Are you ready to be a little more transparent with the Father, who already knows everything?

Do this: Take some time to reflect on the past twenty-four hours and identify a sin or sinful desire that you need to confess to God. Be specific with God about what you did, why you did it, what you should have done, and how you can improve in the future.

Pro tip: Address specific sins, desires, and consequences rather than general pride or sinfulness.

FOURTH | THANK

Continue steadfastly in prayer, being watchful in it with thanksgiving. (Col. 4:2)

Finally, we need to give God our thanks.

Frequently, I devote my entire prayer time to thanking God. I do this deliberately because, like many, I can easily become consumed by asking God for things I want. God wants to hear about the things we want, but he is also worthy of our thanks for the many things he has done.

God loves a grateful man, and while he does not need our gratitude, this does not mean we should not give it to him. In fact, Jesus told a story that directly addresses this issue:

> On the way to Jerusalem he was passing along between Samaria and Galilee. And as he entered a village, he was met by ten lepers, who stood at a distance and lifted up their voices, saying, "Jesus, Master, have mercy on us." When he saw them he said to them, "Go and show yourselves to the priests." And as they went they were cleansed. Then one of them, when he saw that he was healed, turned back, praising God with a loud voice; and he fell on his face at Jesus' feet, giving him thanks. Now he was a Samaritan. Then Jesus answered, "Were not ten cleansed? Where are the nine? Was no one found to return and give praise to God except this foreigner?" And he said to him, "Rise and go your way; your faith has made you well." (Luke 17:11–19)

This is a perfect example of how many people act in their relationships with God in prayer. God is frequently and incessantly generous to man, yet few—in this case, only one out of ten—take the time to give him thanks.

Tell God thanks. Thank him in your time of prayer. When we do this, our minds slow, our hearts submit, joy rises, and our souls find sustenance in God. It's the part of the conversation where we celebrate with God. Our attitude of gratitude keeps us in faithful submission to our graciously giving God.

Do this: Remember to include something you are thankful for in your prayers and tell God thanks—not because he needs to hear it or is sustained by it, but because you need to say it.

Pro tip: From time to time, exclusively thank God in prayer.

PUTTING A PACT TOGETHER

Each of these four components helps shape our prayers when we're in the forge with God. It will take time and practice, but as you repeat them over time, they will become an unconscious part of every prayer. They will help you stoke the fires of prayer and shape your prayers into tools for the Master—and yourself into God's man.

Start hammering these out. Some days, you might focus on only one of these aspects of prayer. That's just fine. Sometimes, you'll need extended time to ask, confess, or thank. However you pray, talk out loud with God. There is no activity more vital in a man's life than the time forged with God in prayer.

> **There is no activity more vital in a man's life than the time forged with God in prayer.**

The longer you practice this rhythm, the more naturally it will continue throughout the day. Your prayer time will evolve, shaping your thinking, informing your actions, and awakening you to the things of God. As you become settled in the daily practice, you will discover that you spend more of your day taking on a prayerful attitude rather than merely utilizing a prayer method.

Notice that Paul wanted the church in Thessalonica to know this kind of life of prayer:

> Rejoice always, pray without ceasing, give thanks in all circumstances; for this is the will of God in Christ Jesus for you. (1 Thess. 5:16–18)

This is my desire for you: a new prayer lifestyle that you can sustain for the rest of your life. If you begin with these four steps, making a PACT with God, over time you will discover a prayer continuity that becomes natural throughout the day. But start with these simple steps, and then add in longer durations and more frequency during the day as you become more proficient. The key is to make it a practice that becomes habitual and easy to repeat. Eventually, the conscious activity will become unconscious, like that last breath you just took.

> Prayer makes a godly man and puts within him the mind of Christ, the mind of humility, of self-surrender, of service, of pity, and of prayer. If we really pray, we will become more like God, or else we will quit praying. (E. M. Bounds)

REFLECTION AND DISCUSSION QUESTIONS

1. Reflect on the acronym PACT (pray aloud, ask, confess, thank) as a prayer framework. How might implementing this pattern enhance your prayer life? Share any experiences or insights you've had with using structured approaches to prayer.

2. Consider the questions raised about prayer in the chapter, such as what to say to God, how to start and finish a prayer, and whether certain topics are taboo. How do these questions resonate with you? Discuss any challenges or uncertainties you've encountered in your own prayer life and how you've navigated them.

THE
TOOL OF
SCRIPTURE

Daily exposure to Scripture forges more opportunities for truth to convict us and shape us.

Walking into a blacksmith's forge is like stepping back in time to an era when craftsmanship and skill took the stage. The sights, sounds, and smells of the workshop create an atmosphere that's both nostalgic and mesmerizing.

When you walk in, you hear the clang of metal against metal, the roar of the fire, and the rhythmic pounding of the hammer as the blacksmith shapes raw metal into something functional and beautiful. It's a symphony of creation, where every strike of the hammer brings the object closer to its final form.

Watching a blacksmith work is like witnessing a mystery unfold before your eyes. You see a lump of metal transformed into a useful tool or work of art, and each hammer blow adds detail and character to the piece. You feel awe and wonder as you watch the blacksmith's rugged hands move with precision and skill, manipulating the metal with seemingly effortless grace.

The popular TV series *Forged in Fire* has captured this for me. It spotlights the art of blacksmithing, showcasing the intense competition and camaraderie among skilled craftsmen.

I'm drawn in by the challenge of forging blades and weapons under pressure and by the sheer craftsmanship and dedication displayed by the contestants.

It connects us to a bygone era. In a world dominated by mass production and automation, blacksmithing remains a deeply human endeavor. There's something primal and elemental about shaping metal with fire and hammer. It's a reminder of our ancestors' ingenuity and resourcefulness.

But it's not just about the process; it's also about the stories behind the craft. Each piece forged in the fire carries with it the blacksmith's skill, creativity, and passion. Whether it's a functional tool or a piece of art, there's a sense of pride and satisfaction in knowing that it was made by hand with care and attention to detail.

In a society obsessed with instant gratification and disposable goods, blacksmithing offers an insightful alternative. It reminds us that crafting a useful tool takes time and effort and that craftsmanship results from hard work and dedication.

Just as the blacksmith carefully crafts metal into a useful and beautiful object, so too does God use Scripture to shape and refine the hearts and minds of men who seek him. The Bible likens Scripture to a double-edged sword, cutting through the noise of the world to reveal truth and wisdom (Heb. 4:12). In the hands of the Master Blacksmith, it becomes a tool for refining character, molding virtues, and sharpening spiritual discernment.

In God's forge, he uses the fire of his Word to soften the hardened places in our hearts. Through the heat of conviction and the light of truth, Scripture exposes our flaws, inviting us to surrender to the transformative work of the Spirit. Scripture shapes us through repetition and practice like the rhythmic pounding of the blacksmith's hammer. Through daily study and meditation, we allow Scripture to sink deep into our souls, reshaping our thoughts, attitudes, and actions. Through discipline and perseverance, we become more like Christ—strong, resilient, and purposeful.

But even when they know the adventure and transformation that awaits them, most men never enter the forge to experience the tool of Scripture. They have a hard time understanding how to use this ancient tool.

The Bible is both inviting and intimidating. It's like a blacksmith's hammer that we're eager to swing. But it's also like a grinding wheel that we are a little scared to submit to. Like the blazing heat of the fire, we are fearful to approach it.

We might buy a Bible—or two, or three—but often, like a prized piece of memorabilia, it sits on the shelf. Nine out of ten US homes possess a Bible, and the average home has about three.[4] But only a very small percentage of men pick it up and read it even once a week. The tool merely sits untouched.

Yet this dust-collecting tool contains the greatest stories ever told. The Bible is filled with love, war, birth, and death. It reveals cultures rich with poetry, history, philosophy, and science. The Bible combines the genres of mystery, romance, suspense, thriller, action, and adventure—and it even contains explicit sexual content.

The Bible has things to say about money. It has things to say about some of the hottest controversies of our time. The Bible boldly dives into conversation topics you carefully avoid at your Thanksgiving table: politics, government, and the church. It is full of hundreds of prophecies that have come true. It contains scientific ideas that very smart people are still trying to understand fully. It describes many archaeological artifacts that we have discovered, thus proving its historical accuracy.

In 1455, the Bible became the first book ever printed on Gutenberg's printing press, and today, it continues to be the bestselling and most-distributed book of all time, with an estimated five billion copies sold. New copies are being produced at a volume of about one hundred million each year. To put those numbers in perspective, the number-two bestselling book of all time is *A Tale of Two Cities* by Charles Dickens, with two hundred million total copies sold and distributed.

Clearly, this tool is worth wielding. But men won't wield it if they are not shown how to use it.

When it comes to the Bible, men are afraid to admit they don't know what to do with it. The very first step stumps them, so they stall out. They are like the stereotypical man who is lost but won't stop to ask for directions. They are too self-sufficient and ashamed. They believe (or hope) they can just figure it out on their own, but they can't. Then, too embarrassed to admit they are lost, they never ask for help. So, they let the tool sit unused on the shelf.

> When it comes to the Bible, men are afraid to admit they don't know what to do with it.

Let's uncomplicate all this by learning what to do and how to use it.

REFLECTION AND DISCUSSION QUESTIONS

1. Reflect on the idea of Scripture being like a blacksmith's tool. How does this comparison enhance your understanding of Scripture's purpose and potential impact on your life? Share any personal experiences or insights you've had of engaging with Scripture as a tool for spiritual growth and transformation.

2. Consider the barriers mentioned that prevent men from engaging with Scripture, such as fear, intimidation, and self-sufficiency. Have you ever experienced similar hesitations or obstacles in approaching Scripture? How have you overcome or addressed these challenges in your journey with reading and studying the Bible?

FOUR INITIAL QUESTIONS ABOUT SCRIPTURE

Those of us who have read Scripture for years forget how challenging Scripture can be when we first begin reading it. Men who are new to Scripture may be unwilling to admit this because they see other believers using it with ease. They don't want to appear ignorant or incompetent, so they won't ask questions—this would reveal their insecurities and might make them look stupid. But men of God push past this concern.

Here are four fundamental questions men ask about the tool of Scripture.

QUESTION ONE | WHICH ONE DO I CHOOSE?

In my lifetime, I have sometimes had the joy of taking a new believer to a local bookstore to pick out his first Bible. This is an exhilarating and insightful event for him. It's like watching a man walk into a forge for the first time. I love the look on his face when he realizes there are hundreds of Bibles to choose from.

On the shelves are study Bibles, archaeological Bibles, devotional Bibles, men's Bibles, patriotic Bibles, teen Bibles, pocket Bibles, and even Word on the Street urban Bibles. Then he usually notices the abbreviations embossed on the sides of the Bibles: NIV (New International Version), ESV (English Standard Version), NLT (New Living Translation), and so on. It's so entertaining to watch his eyes light up with excitement and confusion.

Usually, the man will then look at me and whisper, "Which one?" It's a simple, revealing, and important question that demands an answer.

Scripture was primarily written in two ancient languages: Hebrew for the Old Testament and Greek for the New Testament. Since most of us do not read or speak these languages, the Bible had to be translated into modern languages so it could be easily read. Every English version of the Bible was produced by a team of language scholars who translated the Bible from its original languages. This has been done and redone many times over hundreds of years, for three reasons:

» Languages are always evolving.

» Discoveries are always occurring.

» Approaches are always adapting.

Let me explain.

Did you know that Merriam-Webster added 690 brand-new words, phrases, and acronyms to the dictionary in 2023?[5] This is because language is not static; it is always evolving. Thus, translations from the original Hebrew and Greek into a living, ever-evolving language must adapt with it. In addition, archaeological discoveries are happening all the time. We have made thousands of important biblical discoveries in the last hundred years. For example, the discovery of the Dead Sea Scrolls was one of the greatest biblical discoveries of all time. These ancient scrolls contain text that fortifies (and may even call for new) biblical translations.

But it's the last reason on the list that explains why we see all those versions of the Bible on bookshelves today: translation teams have differing approaches for how they translate the Bible.

When translating Scripture, the scholars doing the work must decide on a translation strategy, goal, and audience. Because some statements in Hebrew or Greek wouldn't make much sense if translated literally into English, the team must decide what to do. Are they going to try to stay as close to the original words and meanings as possible, even if that leaves things a little confusing for today's reader, or are they going to try to guess what the original writer meant and translate that into something the English reader will understand? We can summarize their options into three categories:

» The word-for-word approach (usually translated one word at a time)
» The thought-for-thought approach (usually translated one phrase or thought at a time)
» The paraphrase (usually rendered a paragraph at a time)

Scholars use more technical words for these approaches, but this is a fair summary of their processes. With this, we can now organize all those abbreviations on the sides of Bibles into these three categories.

WORD-FOR-WORD translations like the ESV (English Standard Version), KJV (King James Version), and RSV (Revised Standard Version) all follow this literal-minded format. These translation teams relied as heavily as possible on the original languages, leaving the interpretation work to the reader. Some people like this approach because they would rather study for themselves and dig out the original text and meaning. The drawback is that it can feel awkward or ambiguous to read at times. To get the most from these translations, you need to be willing to learn how to use Bible study tools, like lexicons, to understand the meaning.

Here is an example. A literal, word-for-word translation of the Greek text for Romans 3:22 might read like this: "Righteousness but of God through faith of Jesus of Christ into all the believing. Not for there is distinction."[6]

Got that? Me neither. A literal word-for-word translation is going to read choppy, and most of us need something that reads smoother than that.

A modern English word-for-word translation might translate the text like this: "The righteousness of God through faith in Jesus Christ for all who believe. For there is no distinction" (ESV). Better, but for some, this might still feel a little dense.

THOUGHT-FOR-THOUGHT translations like the NIV (New International Version), NLT (New Living Translation), and GNT (Good News Translation) follow a format that is more reader-friendly. These translation teams attempted to follow a process that conveys meaning for today and is more readable. This means you'll have to trust the translation team more because they have made some interpretations for you. But you shouldn't need to struggle quite as much to understand what you're reading.

Here's an example. A thought-for-thought translation might render Romans 3:22 like this: "This righteousness is given through faith in Jesus Christ to all who believe. There is no difference between Jew and Gentile" (NIV). Much clearer, right? Far less ambiguity. But it's filling in some gaps for you, and sometimes the translators might be a little off in inferring what the original writer meant to say.

PARAPHRASED versions are few. They are just that: a paraphrase. The most popular of these is *The Message*, which was created not by a team but by a single author, Eugene Peterson. It's poetic writing, and Peterson takes a lot of liberty in his rendition. Other paraphrases include The Living Bible (TLB), The Word on the Street Bible, and The Cotton

Patch Bible. Given the subjective interpretation involved, I would not recommend using a paraphrased version for personal study. It's also worth noting that paraphrased translations are less used by the masses, so you may feel out of place using one or reading from one in a group setting.

Here's an example. A passage from a paraphrase might show that the translators have "zoomed out," resulting in a totally different feel to the passage. "Now God says he will accept and acquit us—declare us 'not guilty'—if we trust Jesus Christ to take away our sins. And we all can be saved in this same way, by coming to Christ, no matter who we are or what we have been like" (Rom. 3:22 TLB). This is far more understandable, but it's several steps away from the original text, and unless you know Hebrew or Greek, you would not know this. This is why some feel that paraphrased translations take too much liberty and move too many steps away. But they can be useful for giving you a new perspective on a passage.

Now, back to the earlier question. "Which one?"

For those new to reading the Bible, I suggest the NIV (New International Version) because it is easier to read and understand. An additional benefit of using the NIV is that many preachers reference this translation and it is popular in group settings, which will make it easier for you to follow along with them if you have the same translation.

If you are wondering, I use the ESV (English Standard Version). In fact, I am quoting from the ESV throughout this book. I prefer this version because I want to do some of the translating and interpreting myself. There is meaning here that I want to dig for when I communicate with men. But I have some training in ancient languages and know how to use language-study tools.

In the end, the goal is to find a version that you like and will actually read.

This leads to the next question.

QUESTION TWO | WHERE DO I START READING?

After a man selects the Bible version he wants, his next question is, "Where do I start?"

This is another great question that some men are afraid to ask.

With most books, we start at the beginning and read to the end because they are designed to be read that way. But some books, like dictionaries or cookbooks, we don't read that way. This is also true with the Bible.

The Bible contains sixty-six different books encompassing a variety of literature: romance (Song of Solomon), history (Genesis), religious law (Leviticus), stories of conquest (Joshua), divine drama (Job), prophecy (Isaiah), wisdom (Proverbs), songs (Psalms), written letters (Romans), judgment (Revelation), and narratives of Jesus's life and ministry (Matthew, Mark, Luke, and John). Given this variety of topics and types of literature, we do not necessarily have to start at the beginning. Think of the Bible more like a library—you can skip around and begin reading almost anywhere.

However, my recommendation is to start with one of the four gospels: Matthew, Mark, Luke, or John. *Gospel* means "good news." The four gospels are books of good news containing accounts of Jesus Christ's life and ministry. Each was written by a different author at a different time, which helps you see Jesus's life and ministry from different perspectives.

When a new believer wants an even more specific recommendation, I tend to point him to the gospel of John. In my opinion, it's the most readable retelling of the story of Jesus's life.

Now, though I've said we don't have to read the Bible from front to back, especially when we're new to it, I want to make sure we recognize that the Bible tells a single comprehensive story. The Bible is a compilation of numerous authors writing God's inspired word, each from his own perspective, telling a part of the epic story about God and his Son—Jesus the Savior. It's one book that contains many books that tell one story.

Of course, after reading the gospel of John, you may want to know what to read next. You could go almost anywhere in the Bible, but below is an introduction to the Bible's meta-structure that may help you decide.

QUESTION THREE | WHAT'S WITH THE STRUCTURE OF THE BIBLE?

Think of the Bible as a library with sixty-six books on the shelf. These sixty-six books had forty different authors (though God is the real author behind them all) and were written over a period of about two thousand years.

The Bible is divided into two major sections: the thirty-nine books of the Old Testament and the twenty-seven books of the New Testament. Think of these as part one and part two of God's story. The word *testament* means "a covenant or contract made between God and man," so the Bible contains both the old covenant and the new covenant. Also, the word *old* in *Old Testament* doesn't mean it's no longer valid. The Bible is one long story inspired by God, wholly valid in all its parts. The "old covenant" is valid and fulfilled. It found its fulfillment in Jesus.

> Every storyline in the Bible finds its ultimate culmination in the life, death, and resurrection of Jesus Christ.

The Old Testament is the Hebrew Bible. It's the Scriptures that existed before and during Jesus's lifetime. After Jesus ascended to heaven, the New Testament was composed and added. The life and ministry of Jesus completed the story of God about the Messiah, who was prophesied throughout the Old Testament.

Thanks to those Old Testament prophecies and their fulfillment in the New Testament, we now have one story stretching from the beginning of time to the end narrating the tale of God's love and redemption through his Son, Jesus Christ. The story of Jesus is the meta-narrative that ties all of Scripture together. Every storyline in the Bible finds its ultimate culmination in the life, death, and resurrection of Jesus Christ.

Here is how the sixty-six books are categorized and organized.

The Old Testament (thirty-nine books)
Law: Genesis, Exodus, Leviticus, Numbers, Deuteronomy
History: Joshua, Judges, Ruth, 1–2 Samuel, 1–2 Kings, 1–2 Chronicles, Ezra, Nehemiah, Esther
Poetry/Wisdom: Job, Psalms, Proverbs, Ecclesiastes, Song of Solomon
Prophets: Isaiah, Jeremiah, Lamentations, Ezekiel, Daniel, Hosea, Joel, Amos, Obadiah, Jonah, Micah, Nahum, Habakkuk, Zephaniah, Haggai, Zechariah, Malachi

The New Testament (twenty-seven books)

Gospels: Matthew, Mark, Luke, John

History: Acts

Letters: Romans, 1–2 Corinthians, Galatians, Ephesians, Philippians, Colossians, 1–2 Thessalonians, 1–2 Timothy, Titus, Philemon, Hebrews, James, 1–2 Peter, 1–3 John, Jude

Prophecy: Revelation

This structure will give you a general map for finding the book you might want to read after the gospel of John.

In my opinion, here is one good order to begin reading your Bible:

John: Read John first to get an overview of Jesus's life, works, and key events.

Acts: Read Acts (also called the Acts of the Apostles) second to learn about the early church after Jesus and also to read about Paul's life and ministry, since Paul wrote several books of the New Testament.

Genesis: Read Genesis third to learn the story of creation, humanity, and God's covenant relationship with his people. This is a rewind to the beginning of the Bible and of history. It sets the stage for the unfolding story of redemption throughout the rest of the Bible. Plus, it's a provocative read.

Isaiah: Read Isaiah fourth to learn prophecies about the Messiah and get glimpses into God's redemptive plan. Isaiah lived centuries before Jesus at a time when God's people had turned away from the Lord.

QUESTION FOUR | HOW DOES THIS APPLY TO MY LIFE?

Many men who pick up a Bible discover, almost to their surprise, that it is an ancient historical document from the Near East. The forty authors of its sixty-six books were different from us in time, place, tradition, history, and culture, as were the people they were writing to.

Therefore, sometimes these authors talk about things we don't understand: names, places, events, and traditions. Sometimes we come across cultural nuances that confuse us and complicate the context. Since we don't live in their time or place, we won't understand all the details. This can make interpretation challenging, and at first, it can be difficult to find application to our own lives. This is where many new readers get frustrated and quit, especially those who are trying to read the Bible from front to back.

The core issue we must resolve to effectively read, understand, and apply Scripture is that we don't share the original authors' cultural contexts. However, today, we have a plethora of tools to help us in that task.

It's helpful to learn a reading methodology that is designed with the typical man in mind. Think of such a method as an accessible, repeatable, and convenient tool so a man can read, understand, and apply what he reads. That's my goal: to get you into the Scripture. We're going to turn that book on your shelf from the bestselling but least-read book in the world into the most-read, most-loved book you have ever owned. Remember, to become God's man and live like God's man, you need to hear from the God who made men.

> To become God's man and live like God's man, you need to hear from the God who made men.

REFLECTION AND DISCUSSION QUESTIONS

1. Consider the overwhelming choices new believers face when selecting a Bible. How does the variety of translations and formats contribute to the complexity of engaging with Scripture? Share your thoughts on how this complexity can either facilitate or hinder someone's journey with reading and understanding the Bible.

2. Reflect on the challenge of navigating cultural and historical contexts when reading Scripture. How does the cultural distance between modern readers and ancient authors impact our understanding and application of biblical texts? Discuss methods that could simplify this process and make Scripture more accessible and applicable to men in today's world.

A READING METHOD

In regard to this Great book, I have but to say, it is the best gift God has given to man. All the good the Savior gave to the world was communicated through this book. But for it we could not know right from wrong. All things most desirable for man's welfare, here and hereafter, are to be found portrayed in it.[7] (Abraham Lincoln)

In this section, my goal is to show you how to gain something meaningful from Scripture every time you read it.

In the previous chapter, we discussed the tool of prayer. We learned that the first thing you need to do is determine a time and location. To fully benefit from reading Scripture, you need to do the same thing. You have to carve out a daily slot in your calendar, and you need to select a place suitable for focused reading.

I recommend that you combine the time and place you have allotted for prayer with the time and place for reading Scripture. You should be able to easily add another five to ten minutes to your daily time. Think of these two tools as one complex tool.

Now it's time to add a new acrostic. Last time, we learned PACT, and this time we will learn **PASS**.

> » Pray
> » Author's intent
> » Stop
> » Share

Let's examine these four steps. If you follow them, you will discover some amazing truths while listening to God through his Scripture.

FIRST | PRAY PRIOR TO READING SCRIPTURE

In the beginning was the Word, and the Word was with God, and the Word was God. He was in the beginning with God....

And the Word became flesh and dwelt among us, and we have seen his glory, glory as of the only Son from the Father, full of grace and truth. (John 1:1–2, 14)

There is one major characteristic that differentiates Scripture from every other book in the world, even every other religious holy book. As Hebrews 4:12 says, the Bible is a living document. The Spirit of God indwells it. The very Word of God became a living man in Jesus. Now, Jesus is more than the Bible, and the Bible is not the same thing as Jesus, but the Bible is inhabited by the Spirit of Jesus. The Holy Spirit takes the words of the Bible and uses them in our minds and hearts.

God himself took on human form and walked the earth in the person of Jesus. The fancy word for this is *incarnation*, which means "with flesh." Jesus was God in the flesh. The Bible is called the Word of God, *and* Jesus himself was called the Word of God. The visual here is both strange and significant. Again, the Bible and Jesus are not the same thing. But the fact that they are both referred to as the Word of God conveys the timeless nature of Scripture and the fact that Scripture is enlivened by the Spirit of God. Jesus is the ever-living, ever-present self-disclosure of God's divine language and will.

That is what makes this holy book unique. The Bible is the living revelation by God and about God so we can know God. Scripture is infused with the Holy Spirit of God, who supernaturally reveals truth and is a revelation to those who read it. The Bible is not static writing, like all other books. When we read this book, we're reading living truth that is a revelation from the lips of a timeless God.

> **The Bible is the living revelation by God and about God so we can know God.**

When Jesus arrived on the scene and began his ministry, he testified to everything written and talked about in the Old Testament. He supported its teachings, gave evidence of his authority, and spoke on behalf of God.

> The testimony that I have is greater than that of John. For the works that the Father has given me to accomplish, the very works that I am doing, bear witness about me that the Father has sent me. (John 5:36)

The apostle Paul said this about Scripture:

> All Scripture is breathed out by God and profitable for teaching, for reproof, for correction, and for training in righteousness, that the man of God may be complete, equipped for every good work. (2 Tim. 3:16–17)

Paul described Scripture as the "breath" of God. The Lord "breathed" it out. Scripture is "inspired" by God to use a more modern word. "Inspired" means that it is imbued with God's Spirit. Therefore, Scripture was inspired by God and not by man. Of course, Scripture was *written down* by men. But all men, even the biblical authors, were fallible, sinful, and fallen men like you and me. However, God enabled them to communicate and write down Scripture as directed by him. Thus it's helpful in our lives in four profitable ways:

> » **To teach us:** to show us the path.
> » **To rebuke us:** to show us when we are off the path.
> » **To correct us:** to show us how to get back on the path.
> » **To train us:** to show us how to stay on the path.

Scripture is a powerful supernatural tool, and we should approach it as such. Thus, we need to start with prayer, and since you are already praying at your meeting time and location, reading Scripture should be an intuitive element to add.

But let me clarify something: We start with prayer not because we worship the Bible. People have been known to do that. This is a heresy called *bibliolatry*. We don't worship Scripture. We worship God. But God's Word is razor-sharp. It will teach, rebuke, correct, and train us, and we need to be open to the razor-sharp work it's about to do. We pray in reverence and surrender, recognizing that God does not change, but we do. We realize that the timeless God of the universe will use his timeless Word to teach, rebuke, correct, and train us, carving us into the men he wants us to be.

Prayer prior to reading the Scripture is more about tuning our ears to hear from God than about talking to God. It's a time to become receptive to the divine revelation we are about to receive. Think of this prayer as spadework to the hard, thorny, and rocky soil in your heart that God wants to soften and seed so you will produce greater results.

If you pray prior to reading Scripture, your heart should soften to the message God is about to speak to your soul. If you do this, the results it produces on the other side of reading will be far greater. Don't read the Scripture like you read other books; read it prayerfully.

SECOND | FIND THE AUTHOR'S INTENT

After you have prayed, you're ready to open your Bible. But as you read, you should read a little differently.

Many men begin reading the Bible with the goal of simply getting through a specific number of chapters each day, as when following an annual Bible reading plan. This makes reading the Bible feel like a drudgery. What it really is, is hearing from God. In my opinion, trying to read a target number of chapters is not the best goal, mainly because reading the Bible is not a contest—or a chore.

The better goal is to gain a meaningful understanding of the text you are reading so that it will change how you think and act. With this goal in mind, the amount of text you read is irrelevant. The end goal is change that comes from correct comprehension, not crossing tasks off a list. So let me step you through this.

Let's say you take my advice and start with the gospel of John. I want you to forget about how much you might read in one sitting. Just focus on the words. As you read, always have this question in your mind: *What was the author trying to tell the original audience?*

Here's why this question is so important: the Bible was not written to you.

That's right. This might sound harsh, but it's true. Let me state it again with a small clarification: the Bible was not written to you, but it was written *for* you.

This is why we need to acknowledge the author's original intent. The main audience of each book in the Bible is the person or group to whom it was first written. Let's call them the first audience. Also, each author had a particular reason for writing his book to that first audience.

> **The Bible was not written to you, but it was written *for* you.**

It's this author, this audience, and this message that we need to understand when we read the Bible. We need to understand what the person was originally trying to say and who he was saying it to before we can start thinking about what it might mean for our lives today. Just like a detective looking for clues, we are looking for the author's intent.

For example, when we read John's gospel, we need to understand that John was writing to people of his day. He was recording what he had witnessed, heard, and experienced as he followed Jesus's life, death, and resurrection. I doubt he realized that two thousand years later, people all over the world would be reading his book in thousands of languages.

The global population of the twenty-first century was not John's first audience. Initially, he wanted the people of his day—specifically, believers—to have a record of evidence about Christ, who was both man and God, so that by believing, they might know eternal life. Therefore, when we read it, we need to keep John's original audience and intent in mind.

This principle is the key to understanding what we read and finding a valid application. Without acknowledging the author's intent, we may wrongly interpret the text. Yet when we know the author's intent, our understanding and application will be sounder.

A reader in John's day would have understood him. We can safely assume his readers would have easily caught all his references, nuances, and assumptions and arrived promptly at the intended understanding and personal application. But it's not safe to assume the same for us. Unlike John's early readers, we may have to work to find the author's intent. Therefore, we must attune our attention to his intention. Bible commentaries, Bible dictionaries, and study-Bible notes will help you accomplish this.

THIRD | STOP WHEN YOU ARE CONVICTED

The next step in reading Scripture is to stop when you feel convicted.

As I said before, if you can stop thinking about how much you are reading and focus on what you are reading, the Bible will become life-changing for you. You will find that when you're reading along in Scripture, something will stop you in your tracks. You will experience a moment of conviction or alertness. A verse, or even a few words in a verse, will seem to capture your heart.

When this happens, just stop. What you're experiencing is the living Spirit, who dwells within Scripture, speaking directly to you. Sometimes, this happens after only a few verses; other times, you might be a chapter or two in. You will know when it happens. And when it does, stop.

Just stop.

When I was new to reading Scripture, I would experience moments like this; many times, I would skip right past them because I was trying to get through X number of chapters. But one time, I stopped, stared at the text, read it several times, and even prayed about it. This moment turned into an incredible worship experience between me and God. It was as if God was offering me personal supernatural insights into the world, himself, my life, and my blind spots all at the same time. Why wouldn't I stop to take him up on it? There were so many moments of beautiful instruction from the Lord I had passed up, but not anymore.

> When you're reading Scripture, a verse will capture your heart. When this happens, just stop.

Notice what happened here: I combined two spiritual disciplines, prayer and Scripture. It happened naturally when I was prompted by a conviction of the Holy Spirit. At this moment, I discovered something I had never been taught or encouraged to do by any mentor, teacher, pastor, or leader in my entire life. I discovered that God uses his living Word to speak directly to me to produce change in my life. For many years until that moment, I had ignored these nudges because I was too focused on completing my quota of chapters on that day.

If you stop reading when conviction comes, you will discover new joy and the inspiration of reading the living Scripture. It's far more meaningful than reading a certain number of chapters or consuming a whole book or even the whole Bible without ever experiencing one spiritual change. It's not quantity you are after; it's quality that produces change. Sometimes, reading very small quantities of Scripture will produce quality results in you that deliver the right connection and keep you coming back for more.

Remember, Jesus criticized religious leaders who knew a lot about Scripture but didn't live by its convictions. So, we should focus more on truly listening, understanding, and applying what we read rather than just trying to read a lot.

Notice what Jesus said about the Holy Spirit:

> When he comes, he will convict the world concerning sin and
> righteousness and judgment. (John 16:8)

The combination of God's Word and the conviction of the Spirit has a life-changing impact. If you yield to them, they will transform you. This is precisely what happened to me, and I want it for you. So, as you read, search for the author's intent and await the conviction of the Spirit. When it comes, stop. Don't read one word more. Look to see if the Spirit is giving you one of these three convictions:

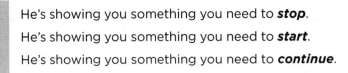

He's showing you something you need to **stop**.
He's showing you something you need to **start**.
He's showing you something you need to **continue**.

This is how I read the Bible today. It takes me longer to read through chapters, but why would I want to read through them faster yet miss the life-changing exercise and life-equipping experience? Take another look at what Paul said to Timothy about the purpose of Scripture:

> All Scripture is breathed out by God and profitable for teaching,
> for reproof, for correction, and for training in righteousness, that

the man of God may be complete, equipped for every good work. (2 Tim. 3:16–17)

Submitting to Scripture is how men become complete and equipped. It's one conviction, one day at a time. Each time we read, may we discover convictions regarding our motives, thoughts, attitudes, and actions. If we read Scripture daily, we are given more opportunities for God's truth to convict us, for his Spirit to work on us, and for his Word to shape us. These daily convictions reveal the proactive steps we need to take to reflect God's glory more perfectly.

FOURTH | YOU NEED TO SHARE IT

After we've prayed, found the author's intent, and stopped when that conviction comes, the last step is to share it.

When men hear me suggest this, some get overwhelmed. I get it. Most think I am asking them to memorize a verse and then stand up to recite it to others. (That is a great idea that's worth the investment of time.) But that is not what I am suggesting. I merely want you to take the principle, truth, or conviction you've gained through reading Scripture and share it with someone else.

Each time you read, try to find something worth telling someone about. Most of the time, what you share will be one of those convictions that stops you dead in your tracks. Other times, it might be a historical learning, a leadership insight, or something you had never noticed before. Regardless, you should carry this into your day, mulling it over.

Find a moment to tell someone about it. Many times, the Lord shows us something in Scripture both to help us and to help someone else. Maybe there's a story or Bible verse you share that ends up being exactly what someone needs to hear that will give them hope. Maybe there's a leadership lesson worth sharing with a leader, peer, or team. Or maybe you need to share that conviction with family, confessing something that needs to change in you.

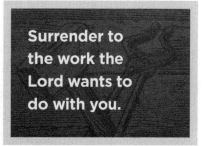

Surrender to the work the Lord wants to do with you.

To make Scripture stick, you can't just read it. You must surrender to the work the Lord wants to do with you through it. You must let it convict and change you, and then you need to communicate it. For some, this step will be easy. Others will have to muster up the nerve. But it's worth the effort. Get after it!

Today, I dare you to find something that captures your attention in a chapter from the Bible. Find a principle worth sharing and then share it. How hard is that? We do it all the time. Today, you probably already talked about that big game yesterday, the latest political gaff, an incompetent leader at work, and that less-than-exciting sermon your pastor preached last week. So go ahead and feel free to discuss something that is more worth sharing—a meaningful Scripture.

DON'T PASS OVER THE OPPORTUNITY

Now it's your turn. Start diving in—not only into prayer, but also into Scripture. Combine them into a single time with God. They are not unconnected disciplines. Let them naturally combine. Pray and read. Then, read and pray.

I practice this daily. You can even do it with me if you like. It's called The Men's Daily Devotional (www.mensdevo.org). In five to ten minutes daily, I use the PASS process mentioned here, working through one book of the Bible at a time. Every devotional time involves these four behaviors: praying, finding the author's intent, stopping when convicted, and sharing it with the world.

Don't pass over Scripture. Instead, be forged and refined by it.

> Is not my word like fire, declares the LORD, and like a hammer that breaks the rock in pieces? (Jer. 23:29)

REFLECTION AND DISCUSSION QUESTIONS

1. Reflect on the significance of starting Bible reading with prayer. How does approaching Scripture prayerfully enhance the reading experience and open yourself to receiving the message God intends? Share examples from your own life where prayer has enriched your engagement with Scripture.

2. Consider the concept of stopping when convicted while reading the Bible. How does this approach differ from simply reading for completion's sake? Discuss the potential impact of pausing and reflecting on personal application when moments of conviction come. Share any experiences where a moment of conviction while reading Scripture led to meaningful change or insight in your life.

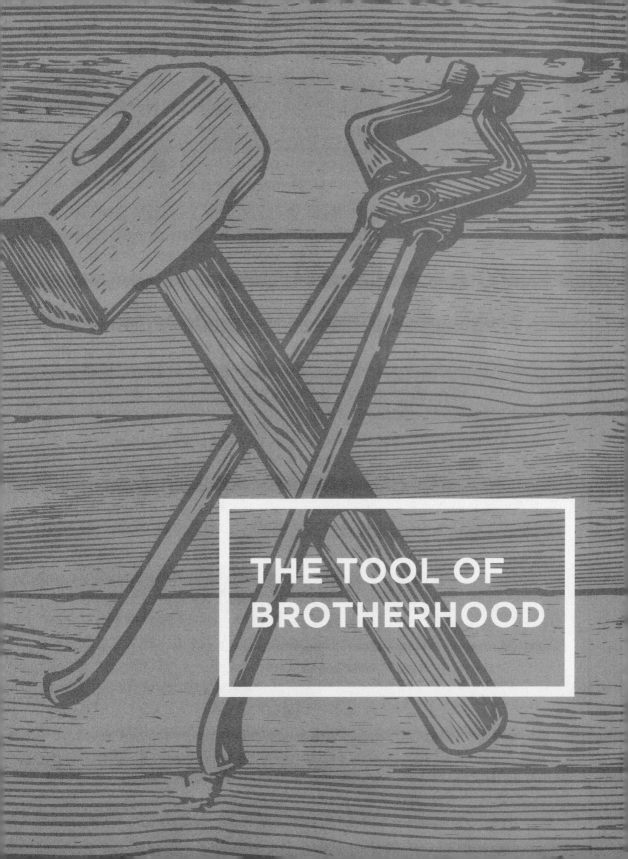

THE TOOL OF
BROTHERHOOD

In the forge of brotherhood, our private disciplines transform into public virtues.

At this point, we will make a shift.

The previous two disciplines are activities we usually exercise on our own. We might call them private or personal disciplines.

However, the next three disciplines—brotherhood, accountability, and ministry—usher the private into the public. There is no way to engage in these privately. Understanding the next discipline, brotherhood, will help with this significantly.

It may sound strange, but brotherhood is far more challenging for men than it should be.

WHAT MAKES BROTHERHOOD SO CHALLENGING?

Navigating the world of male spiritual relationships poses a challenge for many. Men have a mixed-up, messed-up perception of these relationships. The concept of "male spiritual relationships" is unfamiliar and may seem like strange new territory. Even believers may have few meaningful relationships with spiritual brothers. They walk the journey alone, which is a perilous path. Like King David, men who walk alone on the palace rooftop are vulnerable to the allure of all types of lust.

Christian men need to understand that male spiritual relationships are not just nice to have; they are necessary. Yet despite their essential nature, many men don't pursue them. They are usually daunted by the discomfort of taking the initial steps.

Here are four factors that make brotherhood daunting.

FACTOR ONE | MEN DON'T TRUST MEN

All men have baggage when it comes to male relationships. There isn't a man alive who hasn't experienced hurt or harbored some hang-up that hindered his ability to trust certain other males. We've all been disappointed by fathers, friends, pastors, and leaders.

Consequently, we bear wounds. These wounds form scars that act as barriers to our ability to trust others. The prospect of having deeper relationships with men inevitably stirs up past hurts and unresolved issues, serving as a silent deterrent. Wounds inflicted by gossip, aggression, insincerity, manipulation, abuse, or arrogance leave a mark on every man. We think, *Why bother?* It's so much easier to avoid the problems and the pain of the past.

Most men will go to great lengths to avoid any type of potential discomfort—until the pain of doing so becomes so unbearable that it must be addressed. This is how it plays out for most men in the church. Look around. Survey the men's ministry in most churches. Much of their focus is on the pain and problems men encounter: addiction recovery, financial calamity, and marital fallout.

The ministries that serve these pain points for men are crucial, but it's troubling that it takes so much pain for men to try to trust a brother. Many men who participate in these ministries, even for a few weeks, will usually say, "If I'd had a brother and the Bible in my life, I might have avoided all this needless pain." They eventually discover that avoiding brotherhood prolonged the problem and kept them from finding the spiritual solutions God was waiting to provide through other men who have been where they are.

Overcoming our hurts and hang-ups is possible only through the work of Jesus and the power of the indwelling Spirit, but it is accelerated with spiritual brothers. It shouldn't take us so much needless pain and problems to learn this. What believing men need is a more proactive approach.

But to learn to trust a brother, we must learn to love.

Love is the salve for every wound. Love heals the sensitivity of every scar. Our wounds prevent us, but the Lord's wounds heal us.

> A new commandment I give to you, that you love one another: just as I have loved you, you also are to love one another. By this all people will know that you are my disciples, if you have love for one another. (John 13:34–35)

When Jesus gave this new command, he understood what lay ahead for his disciples. He knew trust issues would prevent them from loving one another. Yet, along the way, he modeled love and hoped his men would emulate it.

Our trust issues are resolved with Jesus's love. Declaring our love for a spiritual brother shouldn't feel awkward. Jesus loved his men like brothers appropriately and completely, and he wanted them to love each other in the same way. The reason love is awkward among men is that we don't really let Jesus

To learn to trust a brother, we must learn to love.

love us. Being loved appropriately and completely by Jesus frees us to love others in the same way: appropriately and completely. Many men have never experienced biblical love or had it modeled for them. It's not surprising, then, that they do not know how to love or trust other brothers.

FACTOR TWO | MEN PREFER INDEPENDENCE

Men often hold beliefs about manhood that hinder spiritual brotherhood. One such idea is that masculinity must be rugged, assertive, and independent. This misconception is deeply ingrained and can be found in various forms across different cultures.

Messages that we must be rugged, assertive, and independent men come at us in small sound bites from many sources. Don't believe me? Open a men's magazine, listen to advertising to men, watch any movie marketed to men, or tune into any sports network. Watch and listen to what men say and do. Messages encouraging this version of masculinity are everywhere, regardless of how toxic some proclaim men to be.

But why does this message still prevail?

The simple answer is—men buy it. Godlike, rugged, assertive independence sells. It's everything we want. The same temptation is present in the very first sin, back in Eden: we wanted to be like God, and we still do. It's pointless to blame anyone but our selfish desires. It's nobody's fault but our own. This ideology feeds our selfish pride, and we sell it to ourselves and buy it, too.

Spiritual brotherhood, on the other hand, is a consistent loving attack on our selfish pride. Paul understood this and communicated it this way:

> Love one another with brotherly affection. Outdo one another in showing honor. (Rom. 12:10)

True biblical manhood rescues us from all forms of toxic masculinity. In brotherly love, we discover the need for dependence on God with other brothers. In spiritual brotherhood, we encounter the honor we seek that cannot be known in independence. If you have practical needs, there is a brother who helps. If you are looking for spiritual support, brotherhood is the place.

There are spiritual provisions that can be found only in the company of others: confession, reconciliation, and forgiveness. Each of these is expressed and experienced in brotherhood. Brotherhood is the best pro bono system ever invented. It's where we find every resource we need for the spiritual life. Where better to learn to deactivate our godlike, rugged, assertive independence and activate the spiritual muscle of dependence than with other Christian men?

> **True biblical manhood rescues us from all forms of toxic masculinity.**

It's exciting to see Christian men's groups gathering in cafés, churches, and conference rooms. Whenever I see these groups, I often think that these men are fighting against their desire for independence and discovering the benefits of dependence. They are fighting against the desire for independence within their heart that declares, *I don't need help or a brother.*

FACTOR THREE | MEN ARE TOO BUSY

Some men are too busy and moving too fast to pursue spiritual brothers.

We are moving way too fast, and we know it. From middle-school boys to retired men, the speed of our lives is out of hand. But busyness is a choice. We choose to be overly busy because we prefer to invest our energy and time in the things we are giving our lives to, which we let take precedence over church and brotherhood.

While you may think this is a new problem, it is not.

Let us consider how to stir up one another to love and good works, not neglecting to meet together, as is the habit of some, but encouraging one another, and all the more as you see the Day drawing near. (Heb. 10:24–25)

Notice how the author exhorted this church. He charged them to not neglect regular spiritual meetings and relationships. Clearly, there were plenty of competing demands on their lives. In other words, they were just as busy as we are today. But in this exhortation, he also clarified that the neglect of brotherhood results in missing out on its intended benefits: love, good works, meeting together, and encouragement.

Busyness is an unchanging reality of life. It tempts us to divert more time and attention to things that keep us busy. What I have noticed is that it is right at this point that men punt on spiritual brotherhood. They believe skipping it will give them a little more time, but in the end, all it does is remove them from the spiritual community and spiritual resources that they need more of in busy seasons.

What if *not* giving up on spiritual brotherhood and leaning into it more would uncomplicate and even resolve the busyness of our lives?

FACTOR FOUR | MEN FEAR SPIRITUAL RELATIONSHIPS

The idea of being open, vulnerable, and transparent with other men is unfamiliar and intimidating territory for many men. Just think about it: most of us will prefer to play it safe when the environment is new and the relationships are uncertain. Even if we acknowledge the need for spiritual growth, the actions of building a new relationship with a brother, going to a men's group for the first time, or just attending church can be new and fearful terrain for us.

Many of these inhibitions and fears stem from misconceptions about spiritual brotherhood. Whether they confess it or not, some men view spiritual brotherhood as a sign of weakness, associating it only with support groups where faults, failings, and feelings are the sole subjects discussed. This perception is a fear that has deterred many a man.

> **What if leaning into spiritual brotherhood would actually resolve the busyness of our lives?**

Yet spiritual brotherhood offers much more. It can be a tool that fosters proactive accountability, encouragement, and growth in faith. However, just knowing of these benefits doesn't get men past their fears about the other men in the group, the leader of the group, the place the group meets, and their own lack of spiritual knowledge.

Stepping into spiritual brotherhood for the first time requires courage. It demands a willingness to approach the unexplored fears of the forge and submit to the discomfort that comes with spiritual change.

> Iron sharpens iron,
>> and one man sharpens another. (Prov. 27:17)

This verse graphically captures our grinding fears about male spiritual relationships. We fear the grinder, but we want the shaping and sharpening. Thus, at some point, we have to get beyond our fears and live by faith, subjecting our lives to the sharpening that happens only in the company of other men.

In the end, these are the four factors that make spiritual brotherhood difficult and daunting. But difficult or not, men need brothers. It's a mandate, not an option.

REFLECTION AND DISCUSSION QUESTIONS

1. Reflect on the challenges men face in developing meaningful spiritual brotherhoods. Consider factors such as trust issues, societal perceptions of masculinity, busyness, and fear of change. How have these factors influenced your own experiences with male spiritual relationships? Share any insights or personal stories related to these challenges.

2. Explore the biblical perspective on the importance of brotherhood, as highlighted in the passage from Proverbs 27:17. How does this verse inform your understanding of the benefits and purpose of male spiritual relationships? Discuss practical ways in which men can overcome the challenges discussed in the material to cultivate authentic brotherhoods grounded in faith and mutual support.

ACTIVATE BROTHERHOOD

So, as a brother, let me give you a friendly push toward the starting line with two things you need to do to get moving with the discipline of brotherhood.

ONE | TAKE INITIATIVE

Brotherhood requires initiative from you. Consider this wisdom:

> Again, I saw vanity under the sun: one person who has no other, either son or brother, yet there is no end to all his toil, and his eyes are never satisfied with riches, so that he never asks, "For whom am I toiling and depriving myself of pleasure?" This also is vanity and an unhappy business. (Eccl. 4:7-8)

Life gives us no end of tasks and toil. Men lack meaningful male spiritual relationships because they don't take initiative and because they let life's initiatives act on them.

Building brotherhood requires taking the initiative. No one else can do it for you. It can't be forced by your pastor, accomplished by your wife, arranged by a friend, or mandated by me. Only you can reach out to another man of faith and actively pursue the brotherhood you need.

It's time to assign yourself a task. Pick up the phone or write an email. Don't wait to be invited. Take the first step. Stretch your spiritual muscles and start using

> **Take the first step. Stretch your spiritual muscles and start using them.**

them. I'll provide more guidance shortly, but it's up to you to do something. Take the initiative and stop being reactive and be proactive in your spiritual development.

TWO | THINK SHOULDER-TO-SHOULDER

Now that you have been appropriately encouraged to take initiative, let's try making the ask a little less daunting.

If you are doing this on your own, I know it can be intimidating. If you've never developed a relationship with another believing man, you might be a little overwhelmed right now. The unempathetic side of me says, "Get over it!" But my empathetic side says, "Try to think about it differently."

Think about initiating brotherhood in one of two ways:

1. The ***shoulder-to-shoulder meet-up***, which usually involves an activity.
2. The ***face-to-face meet-up***, which usually involves food and a topic.

The choice is to either (1) do something and talk or (2) eat/drink and talk. Neither option needs much planning, so let's consider what this could look like.

It's often easier to begin with a *shoulder-to-shoulder* activity. It is less intimidating for both of you and gives you something to do while you are building a relationship. It also eliminates all that awkward eye contact. Besides, most men are energized when they are doing something they enjoy. Just invite a guy to come with you to do something that you both like to do.

Think of activities like golf, games, and skeet shooting, where you are standing shoulder-to-shoulder. These activities can be far less intimidating than sitting face-to-face in a coffee shop. There are plenty of shoulder-to-shoulder activities that you probably already enjoy doing with other men, such as bowling, darts, racquetball, or pickleball. Other activities could include service projects, short mission trips, adventure excursions, car repair, shop projects, and hauling junk away.

Shoulder-to-shoulder activities are an easy way to test the relationship and determine whether there is a connection. Your fears about vulnerability and emotional sharing go away because you both know in advance what you will be doing, which will pave the way for other, more vital discussions down the road.

If you're feeling bold, you could suggest meeting up in person for a meal or a drink. Most men will appreciate the invitation, especially if you're treating. However, if you choose this option, it's important to be prepared with things to talk about. You don't want to catch them off guard—that would be awkward.

Next, let's plan what to talk about during both of these meet-ups.

THE 411 ON BROTHERHOOD

> For I have no one like him, who will be genuinely concerned for your welfare. (Phil. 2:20)

This statement from Paul concerns his young disciple Timothy. It's a powerful endorsement from one brother for another. What man doesn't want to have an experience like that? These are the kinds of experiences we want and need with other men in this life.

But to experience this kind of brotherhood, we will have to invest in it and build it. To this end, I want to give you some pointers for structuring your meet-up. They work the same for both types of meet-ups: shoulder-to-shoulder or face-to-face.

But remember, these meet-ups are just like any other meeting you've ever had. Sometimes, we overcomplicate them, believing that spiritual conversations are a lot different or difficult. But let me dispel that idea: spiritual meet-ups are not that different.

FIRST | PREPARE FOUR PURPOSEFUL QUESTIONS

> There was a man of the Pharisees named Nicodemus, a ruler of the Jews. This man came to Jesus by night and said to him, "Rabbi, we know that you are a teacher come from God, for no one can do these signs that you do unless God is with him." (John 3:1–2)

When getting ready for a meet-up with another brother, you don't have to prepare extensively, but you should come up with a few questions in advance. I usually have about four in mind—thoughtful and purposeful questions for the man I will be with, even if I don't end up using them. Here is why.

I have walked away from so many golf outings wishing I had spent more time getting to know the extraordinary men I'd just spent four hours with. This all changed when I prepared for the time by knowing that I was going to have a few intentional conversations. Golf is fun, but it's not the only goal. At some point, the activity should become secondary to the primary reason we are there: spiritual conversations.

You can't let the activity steal the opportunity to make the meet-up purposeful. You can golf, watch a game, or shoot guns while talking about how to raise God-honoring kids, discussing challenges in your marriage, or acknowledging your anxiety about a career change. All this can happen during the activity. Besides, you know you are not a scratch golfer, and a great conversation on hole 7 might be a pleasant distraction from the horrific game you're having.

If you haven't done something like this together before, then prep your buddy on the first tee by saying that you'd like to pick his brain about a couple of topics. This is not out of place to do. Business deals are struck all the time while swinging sticks on a golf course. This just happens to be a spiritual "deal" with eternal implications.

So, what type of man are you meeting with, and what questions do you need to ask? Is he a son or a father? Is he a new friend or an old buddy? Consider the context and person and get ready to build a spiritual relationship.

Here is some language that might help when you've identified who you want to approach and are thinking about how to make the invitation:

> **New Connection Meet-up** (for a man getting to know some-
> one new)
> • I am new to the area. Could we chat about [fill in the blank]?
> • I am navigating [fill in the blank], and I would value your
>   perspective.
> • I heard about your experience with [fill in the blank]. Can
>   we discuss this?

New Believer Meet-up *(for a man beginning his faith journey)*

- I am new to Christ, and I'm seeking wisdom on specific topics.
- I am looking to connect with other Christian men this year; can you point me in the right direction?
- I need some spiritual guidance and thought you might be able to help.

Vocational Meet-up *(for a man looking to make a career change)*

- I am encountering some challenges at work, and I want to pick your brain.
- I am considering a career change and want to learn how you made your transition.
- I'm interested in connecting with Christian men for networking purposes.

Brotherly Meet-up *(for a man looking for consistent relationships)*

- I am looking for one to two guys to connect with on a weekly basis.
- I would like some practical advice on [fill in the blank].
- Would you be willing to grab some coffee a few times?

Urgent Meet-up *(for a man in need of immediate guidance)*

- I am praying about an issue, and I'm not sure what to do.
- I am facing a series of challenges and need some guidance and prayer.
- I heard you have faced similar challenges; can you show me how you overcame them?

SECOND | GET AND GIVE ONE TIP

Therefore encourage one another and build one another up, just as you are doing. (1 Thess. 5:11)

With your four potential questions, you are trying to get (and maybe give) one new tip.

This might feel oversimplified, but it's easy to remember and do. In the context of brotherhood, we aim to become more like Christ and encourage each other toward that end. That's the bottom line. The easiest way to do this is one tip at a time.

With every meet-up, I am aiming to receive something or give something that will pay out spiritual dividends in my life or in his. Preferably, I want to do both. I want to be better for having met with my brother and for him to be better for having spent time with me. Therefore, during the meet-up, I am looking for:

> » A new revelation.
> » An insight into an issue.
> » An encouraging slant on a problem.
> » An opportunity for growth.
> » A chance to encourage my brother.
> » An opening to share something God has revealed to me.

Spiritual conversations can take many unexpected turns. Sometimes, we uncover new insights about the other person, ourselves, or our beliefs. Occasionally, we may learn about all three at once. This is the valuable treasure we seek in our relationships—mutual connection and support.

If the direction of your conversation feels unclear at first, start by getting to know the other guy and asking him about his areas of expertise. Men are well known for liking to talk about themselves! Listen to his experiences in life, relationships, careers, and spiritual journeys. Ask about his faith, family, finances, and fitness. Once you find an interesting topic, focus on it.

Summarize the new insight and express your gratitude for his input. By doing so, you are showing appreciation and letting him know that his words have had an impact on you. This tends to make people light up with happiness. And don't forget, you can share your own insights as well.

THIRD | ADD IN ONE SPIRITUAL ELEMENT

Rejoice always, pray without ceasing, give thanks in all circumstances; for this is the will of God in Christ Jesus for you. (1 Thess. 5:16–18)

Last, we need to add a spiritual element to the meet-up. This is key early in the relationship. Establishing this pattern from the first meeting will serve as a bit of an icebreaker for future meetings. Some men might find this challenging since they have never taken those previous disciplines, prayer and Scripture, public before. If that is the case for you, here is a sample progression scheme that you might think about over your first three meetings with a brother.

> **Meet-up #1: Exchange Prayer Requests**—at the end of the meeting, ask how you can pray for each other.
>
> **Meet-up #2: Pre-Meeting Prayer**—start your second gathering with prayer, keeping it concise yet heartfelt. Witnessing the power of prayer firsthand strengthens bonds and encourages ongoing support. Remember to follow up on previous prayer requests, demonstrating genuine care and commitment.
>
> **Meet-up #3: Prayer and Scripture**—incorporate Scripture into your discussions, sharing passages that connect with you and inviting feedback. This exchange not only deepens your understanding of Scripture but also invites mutual edification and spiritual growth.

It's better to introduce spiritual activity earlier in the relationship than later, because if you put it off for too long, you may never get around to including it. Pierce through the awkwardness of spiritual openness; lean into it.

I call this the "**411 ON BROTHERHOOD**" so that it's easy to recall when you need it:

> » Prepare 4 questions.
> » Get and give 1 tip.
> » Add in 1 spiritual element.

As a final word of encouragement, I'll say that you might not succeed in developing meaningful brotherhood with a first meet-up, and that's okay. Any number of factors can cause problems in the connection, some of which are totally out of your control. There might not be that David-and-Jonathan chemistry in the first meeting (1 Sam. 18). What is important is that you take initiative, work a purposeful plan, and leave the results of the relationship up to God.

Love is the salve for every wound. Love heals the sensitivity of every scar. Our wounds prevent us, but the Lord's wounds heal us.

Building meaningful brotherhood is like forging a sword. Just as a blacksmith meticulously crafts each blade, heating, shaping, and tempering it, so too must you invest time and effort into forging deep connections. If the metal of the relationship fails to take the right shape on the first try, it's not a failure—it's an opportunity to refine your technique. Reflect on what didn't quite click, and then adjust your approach and seek out another brother whose life connects with yours. The key is to not give up, because spiritual brothers make us sharper in this life, and we need each other. I need you, and you need me.

REFLECTION AND DISCUSSION QUESTIONS

1. Reflect on the concept of taking initiative in brotherhood. How does the idea resonate with you that meaningful male spiritual relationships require personal initiative? Have you ever taken the initiative to reach out to another man for the purpose of cultivating spiritual brotherhood? If so, what was your experience like? If not, what barriers or hesitations have prevented you from doing so?

2. Consider the practical suggestions provided for initiating and structuring brotherhood meet-ups, such as the shoulder-to-shoulder and face-to-face approaches. Which approach do you find more appealing or suitable for your personality and preferences? How might you apply the "411 on Brotherhood" framework in your own efforts to establish and nurture meaningful relationships with other Christian men? Share any insights or plans for action based on these strategies.

THE TOOL OF
ACCOUNTABILITY

In the forge of accountability, wisdom is honed, courage is forged, and character is refined.

> The way of a fool is right in his own eyes,
>> but a wise man listens to advice. (Prov. 12:15)

Accountability accelerates spiritual growth in a man.

If you read deep into the verse above, you will see the benefits and beauty of accountability that most men miss. Read it again.

Accountability brings us into a relationship. It shapes and sharpens our wisdom. It refines foolish ideas and decisions. It forges courage for challenging times where previously there was none. It refines character. But the real benefit we tend to overlook is the awareness it provides that can move us more rapidly from foolishness to wisdom.

In our culture, men aren't usually encouraged to seek help. We're told to "man up." Therefore, we try to handle life alone, often leading to foolishness and sin. What we really need is the support of brothers and accountability. Here's why:

> I tell you, on the day of judgment people will give account for every
> careless word they speak. (Matt. 12:36)

Accountability is inevitable. It's an undeniable reality. We can't dodge or duck it. Eventually, all men will stand before the throne of God to give an account of their actions in this life.

Accountability gives us the ultimate pay-now or pay-later choice. Every follower should want to be more proactive and less reactive. When it comes to our actions and choices, we should pay now in the forge so we don't have to pay later in life or in eternity.

> The awareness accountability provides can move us more rapidly from foolishness to wisdom.

Think about it. Why not endure the shame of being called out today so we don't get shafted tomorrow? Why not be called out by a brother in private rather than being called out before a crowd? Why not submit to the correction of a leader rather than be canned from a career job? Why not endure humiliation by a drill sergeant rather than endure humiliation and loss in battle?

To me, a little momentary distress sounds a lot better than long-term loss or embarrassment. This is the wisdom of accountability. Practice paying up now or get ready to pay up more later. So why not invite a brother you trust to help you stay on course? You can't avoid it anyway, and in the end, it will make you more wise and less foolish.

MEN HAVE TROUBLE WITH ACCOUNTABILITY

If you work in a high-accountability environment, you know that accountability works.

I have a few friends who work in strictly managed occupations and whose daily actions are monitored carefully by numerous people. Most of these friends work in settings that protect and care for human life. It might sound burdensome to us, but those who excel welcome and invite accountability. They know that appropriate accountability leads to better outcomes, especially when lives are on the line.

In a spiritual context, seeking accountability for our actions and motivations can feel daunting. Therefore, we resist it. Maybe because:

> » We are fiercely independent.
> » We are afraid of being exposed.
> » We have had bad experiences with accountability.
> » We don't know how to invite it.
> » We don't want to appear weak.
> » We don't really want to change.
> » We believe we are accountable only to God.

I have heard every one of these excuses from men, and I'm guilty of having said a few myself. But all our troubles boil down to one big issue. It's not an issue with the purpose, the process, or the people. It's an issue with us. We simply harbor too many bad beliefs and attitudes about Christian accountability.

So let's look at two things you are going to have to do first to open yourself to accountability: ditching bad beliefs and attitudes, and learning how to give and receive positive spiritual accountability.

DITCH THE BAD BELIEFS AND ATTITUDES, AND LEARN POSITIVE SPIRITUAL ACCOUNTABILITY

You hypocrite, first take the log out of your own eye, and then you will see clearly to take the speck out of your brother's eye. (Matt. 7:5)

Men have deep-seated misconceptions about spiritual accountability, which is why they are often reluctant to offer it or to accept it.

Many men harbor hurts and hang-ups associated with accountability gone awry. Some have been wounded by fellow brothers who exploited trust and manipulated situations for their own gain. As a result, we're understandably wary of subjecting ourselves to potential harm or perpetuating the same harmful patterns we've endured.

> **What's so ironic about this is how we eagerly enjoy accountability when someone else receives it.**

What's so ironic about this is how we eagerly enjoy accountability when someone else receives it. We celebrate when that guy who cut us off in traffic gets pulled over a mile up the road (or at least we enjoy imagining that outcome). We cheer and jeer when a player we dislike is penalized or benched, allowing our team to secure a victory. We party, parade, and post when that deceitful, manipulative, narcissistic leader finally gets busted. Deep down, we secretly enjoy accountability—but only when it happens to other people.

In Christian circles, accountability is mainly expressed in the context of sin and addiction. You've probably noticed the abundance of resources aimed at men dealing with sexual and chemical addiction in recent years. While it's true that accountability can be helpful in breaking free from addiction, we've got to see the blessing of accountability in the bigger picture.

> **Accountability is not just an aid for addressing addiction and sin; it's also an aid for spiritual growth.**

Accountability is not just an aid for addressing addiction and sin; it's also an aid for spiritual growth that goes beyond behavior modification.

Accountability can be powerful, positive, proactive, and preventative. Consider the accountability you witness between a seasoned coach and an aspiring athlete. Everything this coach does is about accountability aimed at making a player better so they can win together. A coach is training, preparing, leading, building, and, on some occasions, tearing down. Great coaches understand that reactive accountability will have diminishing returns. So, he must work to find an approach that's right for the athlete under his charge. The goal is *proactive* accountability to build him into a better player so they have a better team and they can win on the field of play together.

Now, let's apply this to spiritual accountability. The intent of accountability should be to make us better men, fathers, husbands, and leaders. It should be powerful, positive, proactive, and preventative. Accountability is not exclusively a tool to ward off sin by rebuke and correction; it's also a tool to train us to become the men God wants us to be.

> All Scripture is breathed out by God and profitable for teaching, for reproof, for correction, and for training in righteousness, that the man of God may be complete, equipped for every good work. (2 Tim. 3:16–17)

But what does this positive side of accountability look like?

Well, it challenges us to receive and accept more of God's grace, forgiveness, love, and mercy. It persuades us to pray, read Scripture, build brotherhood, and engage in ministry more effectively. It can encourage godly action with your wife, children, friends, and peers. But to step into it, you need to get past bad beliefs and attitudes.

> Iron sharpens iron,
>> and one man sharpens another.
>>> (Prov. 27:17)

The iconic men's ministry verse again. To know the meaning of this scripture, you need to get past the memorization of it and learn to love the process it prescribes. When iron sharpens iron, a wheel is grinding, sparks are flying, and the room is filled with the shriek of iron-on-iron rub. The sounds and sensations of this grind can be painful. It's what we must endure to achieve a sharpened instrument.

The rough spots that men need to grind away with accountability are all our bad beliefs and bad attitudes about the concept. If you don't grind these off, you'll end up doing nothing, and unused iron does only one thing: it rusts.

It's time to grind off all those bad beliefs and attitudes. Go ahead and write them down for your own personal awareness. Start including them in your prayer time as part of a confession to yourself and to God. For example, you could say something like:

> God, I have lived in isolation for far too long.
> God, I've harbored a suspicious attitude toward Christian men in general.
> God, I'm afraid of being exposed. There are sins in my life that I'm not ready to confess to others.
> God, I feel overwhelmed by the mistakes I've made.
> God, I worry I won't feel accepted by the men of my church.
> God, I'm afraid of change.
> God, I've been wounded by past experiences with accountability.
> God, I fear appearing weak by attending that group.

To get going, you need to ditch all this garbage and welcome the joy of a new perspective. Listen to James:

> Count it all joy, my brothers, when you meet trials of various kinds, for you know that the testing of your faith produces steadfastness. And let steadfastness have its full effect, that you may be perfect and complete, lacking in nothing. (James 1:2–4)

Instead of focusing on these bad beliefs and attitudes, all of which stem from fear and lead to "rusty" lives, embrace the joy of persevering faith, and realize all the potential good outcomes. Look beyond the pain to the perfect work that produces perseverance and perfection in you.

If you can get rid of these beliefs and attitudes, you will discover a new approach to accountability that will result in a joyful experience.

REFLECTION AND DISCUSSION QUESTIONS

1. Reflect on the barriers to embracing accountability outlined in the text, such as fear of exposure, past negative experiences, and a desire to maintain independence. Have you encountered any of these barriers in your own journey of faith? How have these barriers hindered your ability to engage in meaningful accountability relationships? Discuss strategies that can help overcome these barriers and foster a more receptive attitude toward accountability.

2. Consider the concept of positive, proactive spiritual accountability as described in the text. How does this perspective challenge traditional views of accountability, which are primarily focused on addressing sin and addiction? Reflect on the potential benefits of proactive accountability in fostering personal growth, spiritual development, and relational support. Share examples of how proactive accountability can be implemented in practical ways within Christian communities to promote mutual encouragement, learning, and empowerment.

PRELIMINARIES FOR POSITIVE ACCOUNTABILITY

Now for two preliminary activities that lead to positive and proactive accountability.

ONE | DETERMINE ONE AREA THAT YOU WANT TO IMPROVE

Let no one despise you for your youth, but set the believers an example in speech, in conduct, in love, in faith, in purity. (1 Tim. 4:12)

Accountability necessitates setting a goal. In the verse above, Paul gave his disciple Timothy some areas to consider: speech, conduct, love, faith, and purity. Paul knew Timothy well enough to understand how to help him along. If you read through First and Second Timothy, you will see these are precisely the points where Timothy needs positive accountability.

What about you? Where could you use some positive and proactive accountability?

Most men never stop to think about this in their spiritual life. In fact, most men never even set spiritual goals. But we should. We should set goals in our spiritual life as we do in every other area of life. I set three specific spiritual goals every year. And over the years, they have contributed to profound advancements in my spiritual growth.

> **Most men never set spiritual goals. But we should.**

If you have not done this before, don't bite off too much your first time. Simply identify one area to target.

For example, you could target your marriage, a spiritual discipline, family spiritual leadership, evangelism, or merely the kind of language you use. Once you know the area, determine one specific and measurable goal that you would like to achieve over the next year.

Don't forget: if you try to do too many things or too much, you will end up being overwhelmed or diluting your focus, which will likely cause you to either overlook something or fail entirely. Set yourself up for success by making your first spiritual goal achievable so you can feel the win, and then scale up next time.

If you have already done this, then determining one area to improve is going to be easy. Either way, take a moment to write down your spiritual goal below. In three to five words, identify one area you want to improve (and keep it positive):

TWO | DESCRIBE THE OUTCOME OF THE GOAL

After you have suffered a little while, the God of all grace, who has called you to his eternal glory in Christ, will himself restore, confirm, strengthen, and establish you. (1 Pet. 5:10)

Peter understood that there is a purpose in suffering. We don't always see it when we are in it, but it's there. Sometimes, it is painful. But the best part of proactive and positive accountability is that we get to visualize and describe the outcome of the goal. We can endure the pain because we know it has a purpose.

I want you to visualize the ideal outcome of your goal. Take the goal you wrote down above and imagine how you and your life would look differently if you accomplished it. I want you to picture how your life would be "restored, confirmed, strengthened, and established," as Peter talked about above.

> There is a purpose in suffering. We don't always see it, but it's there.

Consider this one question: *How would my life be different if I were successful in reaching this spiritual goal?*

Reflect for a minute and imagine it before you write it out. Think about how your motives and desires would be different. Imagine the changes in your character. Visualize what behaviors would change. Consider how success would affect those around you. Then, in a few sentences, describe the new you.

These two preliminary steps—determining one area and describing the outcome—are critical. Without them, you cannot move forward and effectively engage in accountability that produces results. But once you have done these, the next steps are much easier.

DO ACCOUNTABILITY

Now it's time to do accountability. *Declare* it and *own* it. Or DO it.

FIRST | DECLARE IT

But the Lord said to [Ananias], "Go, for [Paul] is a chosen instrument of mine to carry my name before the Gentiles and kings and the children of Israel." (Acts 9:15)

When he who had set me apart before I was born, and who called me by his grace, was pleased to reveal his Son to me, in order that I might preach him among the Gentiles. (Gal. 1:15–16)

> The Lord stood by me and strengthened me, so that through me the message might be fully proclaimed and all the Gentiles might hear it. (2 Tim. 4:17)

The apostle Paul was given a clear call. His life calling was to preach the gospel to Gentiles (i.e., non-Jewish people). From the time of his conversion to the day of his death, he was faithful to this call. It was declared over him and declared by him. By this public declaration, he was held to account and was accountable all his days. This declaration was his entire defense throughout the New Testament.

How would your life be different if you were successful in reaching this spiritual goal?

Great men make great declarations. It's time to declare what you have determined and described above. Since you now know what you want to do, taking the next step is easy. All you need to do is publicly declare it.

Don't wait too long to announce your intent. Share your goal and desired outcome with someone. If you've taken up the challenge of the last chapter, you could declare this to the brother you are meeting up with. You could also declare it to a spouse, friend, or family member. If you want to be bold, declare it on social media. The point is to get it out there.

Your public declaration is important for two reasons. First, when you proclaim your goal publicly, you are pledging yourself to action. Second, when social accountability accompanies your declarations, it puts pressure on you. If you have truly addressed those bad beliefs and attitudes, then this step becomes easier. The pressure to live up to your word will help you integrate your goal into your public and private life.

Great men make great declarations. It's time to declare what you have determined.

In a sense, declaring your goal publicly helps others help you. When people know what you are trying to do, they can root for you, inquire about progress, and pray for the outcome you seek. It's powerful and effective! If you want results, don't keep the goal and outcome private; declare it publicly.

SECOND | OWN IT

Let each one test his own work, and then his reason to boast will be in himself alone and not in his neighbor. For each will have to bear his own load. (Gal. 6:4–5)

You need to declare your need for change and then own it. Accountability is 100 percent your responsibility.

Proactive accountability works best when it's owned by you. Reactive accountability is typically owned by others, mainly because another system or party is trying to force a behavioral change upon you. But while positive and proactive accountability may benefit from motivation from another party, as we've seen, it primarily demands your motivation and your action.

This is often why believers have such bad experiences with accountability relationships. We expect someone else to provide all the motivation, training, and effort and do the heavy lifting in holding us accountable. This sounds more like in-patient therapy. In extreme cases, it is necessary, but most men in churches today simply need a more brotherly approach.

Here's a game changer in accountability: you need to own the process. You determine the goal, describe the outcome, declare your intent, and then take responsibility for check-ins. You are taking the initiative all the way through to the end. You are responsible for initiating conversations in which you tell the truth about what's going on in your growth process.

Accountability works only when you want it and when you pursue it. Nobody can corner you into the sort of honesty that leads to change. You must be willing to set a goal, willing to change, willing to get help, and willing to invite check-ins. It's time to own it.

And here's one additional note. Own the initiative to *schedule* regular check-ins and share your progress with a brother. This is easier than we make it. Through texts or calls, or at the top of a face-to-face meeting, do a check-in on your goal on three key topics:

> » What you need to *start* doing.
> » What you need to *stop* doing.
> » What you need to **continue** doing.

It's time to forge a bond of accountability. Accountability will involve heat, pressure, and molding. Deep inside the fire of honesty and vulnerability, we'll discover impurities that need to be refined and weaknesses that need to be strengthened.

So, let's dive deep into the forge of accountability, my friend. Let's embrace the heat, the pressure, and the transformation that come from walking this journey together. And as we emerge from the fire, may we be stronger, sharper, and more resilient than ever before.

Let's DO it together.

> You must be willing to set a goal, to change, get help, and to invite check-ins. It's time to own it.

REFLECTION AND DISCUSSION QUESTIONS

1. Reflect on the importance of setting a spiritual goal and describing its potential outcome, as outlined in the text. Why is it essential to identify one area for improvement and envision how achieving this goal would impact your life? Share a personal experience of setting a goal and describing its desired outcome. How did this process influence your approach to accountability and personal growth?

2. Discuss the significance of declaring and owning accountability in spiritual development. Why is it crucial for individuals to publicly declare their goals and take full ownership of their journey toward growth? Share examples of how declaring accountability publicly and taking personal responsibility can lead to positive outcomes and transformation. How can individuals proactively engage in accountability check-ins and cultivate a mindset of continuous improvement?

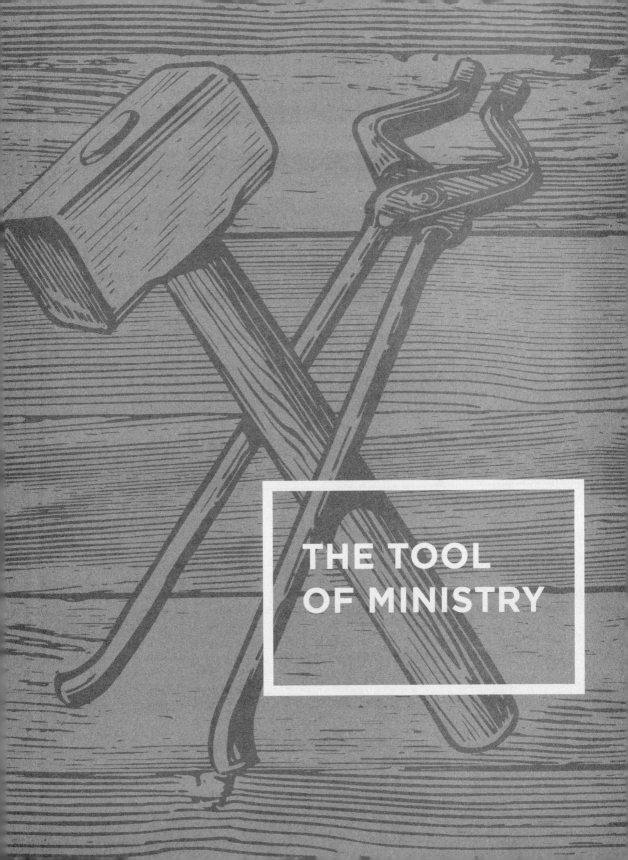

THE TOOL
OF MINISTRY

Ministry is not exclusively for professionals.
In fact, it is not even optional. It's mandated.

Ministry is the last of the five disciplines, and it is the one I find to be the most motivating for men.

Men were designed to act, to get things done, to produce, and to find creative ways to use the restless energy God gave us. We were created with a purpose, and that purpose is to join God in his work and act as his representative wherever we go and in whatever we do.

What incredible responsibility!

MINISTRY IS OVERWHELMING

If you have ever stepped into a blacksmith's workshop, you know it can be an overwhelming experience. But it's even more overwhelming to do it. The tools are simple, but blacksmithing is a craft that involves shaping and manipulating hot metal using several techniques. The principles involved in forging, such as hammering, bending, twisting, and drawing out, take a long time to master. Beginners struggle with achieving the desired shapes and forms in their metalwork until they gain more experience. The work is far more mentally and physically demanding than most people expect.

Many men feel the same way about doing ministry. They know all men are supposed to do it, but there are factors that make it seem as overwhelming as entering a blacksmith's workshop. Here are three of those factors.

FACTOR ONE | UNDERSTANDING MY DESIGN

We are his workmanship, created in Christ Jesus for good works, which God prepared beforehand, that we should walk in them. (Eph. 2:10)

You have probably been told this, but many find it elusive: God made you with intent and for a purpose. But one of the great challenges in our journey is making sense of this design. As men, we have this insatiable drive to live purposeful lives. Yet as we begin our spiritual journey, it feels just as mysterious and as overwhelming as stepping into a blacksmith's workshop. Our purpose was put into the forge to shape it in the Master Blacksmith's design. While this experience is new, exhilarating, and full of anticipation, it can be overwhelming.

We are in process. We are the "workmanship" of God. We are individually and intentionally created by God in the divine forge. Each of us is a one-of-a-kind product formed by the hand of God. And while we await an understanding of this design and purpose, this doesn't change the reality of God's intent: he crafted us with purpose and for a purpose.

We know with confidence that he created us "for good works." You can be sure of this. Your design—made manifest through your talents, gifts, and abilities—is direct evidence of your purpose: to channel everything you are into his "good works." These works are your ministry.

Paul went even further by declaring that God prepared these works for us beforehand, which is reassuring. With this forward look of God, we anticipate what God might do with us in the future. But even more, we should stop and consider all the divine circumstances that have brought us to this very moment. Consider it right now: all the divine providence that has led you to this specific moment in time. Think about everything God has already revealed about his workmanship of you, because this declares what God has purposed for your future.

> **Your talents, gifts, and abilities are your ministry.**

Your purpose and design can feel elusive, and pinpointing it can seem difficult. But it's not actually as elusive as you think. We will clarify this a little later, but for now, don't be deterred: God wants you to discover and steward the good works, the ministry, he has called you to do.

FACTOR TWO | UNDERSTANDING MY FIT IN THE CHURCH

For just as the body is one and has many members, and all the members of the body, though many, are one body, so it is with Christ....

The eye cannot say to the hand, "I have no need of you," nor again the head to the feet, "I have no need of you." On the contrary, the parts of the body that seem to be weaker are indispensable, and on those parts of the body that we think less honorable we bestow the greater honor, and our unpresentable parts are treated with greater modesty, which our more presentable parts do not require. But God has so composed the body, giving greater honor to the part that lacked it, that there may be no division in the body, but that the members may have the same care for one another. If one member suffers, all suffer together; if one member is honored, all rejoice together.

Now you are the body of Christ and individually members of it. (1 Cor. 12:12, 21–27)

The second factor that can be overwhelming is understanding our purpose and fit in the church.

Some men express deep frustrations with the church. I've listened to countless complaints, challenges, and concerns stemming from a genuine desire to see the church thrive. Men long to experience the church at its best, to connect with a community, to support it, to invite others into it, and, above all, to find their meaningful place within it. But they don't always succeed in doing so.

The church is of immense importance to believers. Therefore, we must acknowledge that avoiding or disregarding our involvement in it isn't an option. Worshipping together and engaging in ministry as a community are vital to our faith and growth.

However, navigating our role within the church can be as complex as understanding the workings of the forge. It looks simple, but simple it is not. We may struggle at times to see how we fit in the picture, particularly when entering a new congregation. It's common to feel like everyone except us has a place and purpose there. Yet even in our discouragement, we can find some comfort in knowing that the early church faced similar challenges, as evidenced in the text above.

Even in the church's infancy, men grappled with frustrations within it. However, Paul emphasizes that we cannot simply give up on the church or our personal involvement in it. Despite the difficulty in discerning our place, we must push through these challenges. Why? Because the body cannot function effectively without every member participating. Just as we need the body, the body needs us. It's crucial to recognize that our talents, abilities, and gifts were given to us not for selfish purposes but for the greater good. Therefore, we should generously invest them in others within our church community to accomplish greater deeds together.

If we disengage from the church, not only does the church miss out on our contribution, but we also miss out on the opportunity to grow and thrive. In essence, everyone loses.

I know so many brothers who resist joining the church not because of a stubborn streak, but due to previous painful experiences. Trust me, I get it. And I agree that the church is full of flawed men. But that should surprise no one because every church is made up of flawed, fallen men just like you and me. Even so, the church is still God's method of choice for demonstrating his love to the world.

Never forget that Jesus loves his church. Enough to lay down his life for it. Therefore, we must struggle through this complication, even as we are trying to find our fit in the church. It may take years for us to find it. We might have to endure staffing issues, small-group problems, grotesque sins, and even theological disagreement, but the body will ultimately function better if we can push through the complicating issues.

FACTOR THREE | THE VOICE OF SELF-DISQUALIFICATION

If the foot should say, "Because I am not a hand, I do not belong to the body," that would not make it any less a part of the body. And if the ear should say, "Because I am not an eye, I do not belong to the body," that would not make it any less a part of the body. If the whole body were an eye, where would be the sense of hearing? If the whole body were an ear, where would be the sense of smell? But as it is, God arranged the members in the body, each one of them, as he chose. If all were a single member, where would the body be? As it is, there are many parts, yet one body. (1 Cor. 12:15–20)

This highlights another big factor for men: self-disqualification.

Men often think they are not good enough to serve in ministry—not educated enough, not knowledgeable enough, too immature, too young, too old, or too used up. They think their inability to teach, their weakness as a leader, or their lack of a title means they can't participate in ministry meaningfully. Men will always feel they need a little more experience, more permission, and more support. These voices of negative self-talk create a void for men who are needed in the church.

This needs to stop because it is stopping so many great men.

Now, let's understand that sometimes events can disqualify a man from official church leadership. But this would not disqualify him from doing ministry. If the Holy Spirit lives within you, this is all the qualification you need to do God's good work. The voice of self-disqualification is not of God. Most of the time it contradicts the truth from God, who has designed you for purpose and equipped you with the Spirit to carry it out.

> When they saw the boldness of Peter and John, and perceived that they were uneducated, common men, they were astonished. And they recognized that they had been with Jesus. (Acts 4:13)

Look at Peter and John. I bet they heard the voice of self-disqualification. Even the crowd deemed them uneducated, common, and underqualified. But when empowered by God, their "uneducated" approach illuminated their action, and observers saw their boldness. Do you want evidence that God can do anything with any man, even the common man? Then look at Peter and John.

> If the Holy Spirit lives within you, this is all the qualification you need to do God's good work.

When a man courageously resists the voice of self-disqualification, God can do more in and through him than any man can on his own. As the man acts in obedience, God does something astonishing.

Ministry work follows a different set of rules than what we're used to in the "work" world. In most vocations, you need a vast education, a lot of preparation, and even permission. Ministry doesn't play by these rules. While we should be educated in God's Word, preparing our hearts in prayer, and receiving training to minister, these are all secondary to acting in faith and doing daily ministry.

God is merely looking for faithful and obedient men. Through this, God does the work we cannot do—he draws men, changes hearts, and heals people. The things he does through us are greater than anything we could do of our ability. While you will always find personal enrichment in the pursuit of education, training, and affirmation, these have no bearing on the spiritual aspect of what God is able to do through common and uneducated men who have been with Jesus.

> He who calls you is faithful; he will surely do it. (1 Thess. 5:24)

Here is a great Old Testament moment that illustrates this point. King David was handing the leadership baton off to his son Solomon, who was soon to be king. David was, for many reasons, qualified to conquer the land and be king, but God had specifically forbidden him from building a Temple. However, David did not allow this prohibition to stop him from laying the groundwork. The Bible records that David gathered every possible resource the Temple's construction would require.

David honored God's instruction and stopped short of construction itself while doing everything he was qualified to do. He didn't sit in the corner and sob because he was disqualified from one specific act; instead, he did everything possible to support the process. He gathered every necessary ounce of gold and silver, every stone, and every plank of wood. He hired the workers. He established the leadership infrastructure. He developed the plans and their scope and sequence with God's help. Once everything was in order, David handed it to his son.

> David said to Solomon his son, "Be strong and courageous and do it. Do not be afraid and do not be dismayed, for the LORD God, even my God, is with you. He will not leave you or forsake you, until all the work for the service of the house of the LORD is finished. (1 Chron. 28:20)

Solomon needed only strong faith and courage. Nothing more. Talk about succession planning. Everything had been done for him by his father. Here, David silenced Solomon's voice of self-disqualification, which could have kept him from accomplishing the task.

In the same way, our Father has gathered up endless resources. He's done all the ground-work. He's defeated sin and death. He's extended limitless grace, mercy, forgiveness, and love. He's given us the Spirit. He's even given us gifts of the Spirit.

He's given everything … and then we reject it all by listening to a devious voice preaching in our heads? Preposterous.

God wants to do work in and through you right now. Don't allow the voice of guilt, shame, and fear to paralyze you. You may feel you have no talents, abilities, or gifts to speak of, but this is a misperception about you and God. If you are born again, you are born ready, endowed with power. Self-disqualifying thoughts and beliefs are your first obstacle. God will clarify the next steps. All you must do is silence the self-disqualification of your own voice. As soon as you hurdle this obstacle, you'll gain momentum and discover this fact: God calls us and equips us along the way.

> To those who are called, both Jews and Greeks, Christ the power of God and the wisdom of God. For the foolishness of God is wiser than men, and the weakness of God is stronger than men. (1 Cor. 1:24–25)

REFLECTION AND DISCUSSION QUESTIONS

1. Reflect on the concept of understanding one's design and fit within the church, as discussed in the text. How do you perceive your unique purpose and role within God's plan? Share any challenges or difficulties you've faced in discerning your purpose and fitting into the church community. How can recognizing and embracing your God-given design enhance your ministry and contribution to the body of Christ?

2. Discuss the issue of self-disqualification among men in ministry. Why do many men struggle with feelings of inadequacy and self-doubt when it comes to serving in the church? Share personal experiences or observations of how self-disqualification has hindered ministry opportunities. How can individuals overcome these negative voices and step into their calling with courage and confidence?

YOU HAVE BEEN REPURPOSED

He gave the apostles, the prophets, the evangelists, the shepherds and teachers, to equip the saints for the work of ministry, for building up the body of Christ, until we all attain to the unity of the faith and of the knowledge of the Son of God, to mature manhood, to the measure of the stature of the fullness of Christ. (Eph. 4:11–13)

Understanding our design, discovering our fit, and overcoming self-disqualification are crucial steps in addressing some of the initial factors men face with ministry. However, beyond these factors lies the need to better understand what ministry entails. Fundamentally, ministry boils down to the actions of a man committed to living out his faith in godly ways.

Ministry is the believer's way of life.

Many of us are overwhelmed by the proposition of ministry because we separate our daily life from our faith. While we readily embrace Jesus as our Savior, the idea of him being the Lord of our everyday life is far more challenging. Surrendering to his lordship implies significant changes and a new life perspective. Our life after surrendering to his lordship should look different from how it was before.

I understand why believing men disconnect their regular lives from the call to ministry. First, our perspective of ministry involves pastors or church staff who are paid to lead, teach, and care for the church. Consequently, we perceive ministry as something reserved exclusively for those in paid or professional roles within the church, overlooking the fact that all believers are called to ministry.

> **Ministry is the believer's way of life.**

Second, some believe that because they are engaged in vocations outside of ministry, they can postpone their involvement in ministry at the church until their career is done. In the meantime, they focus on their jobs and providing for their families, assuming ministry can wait.

However, both are huge misconceptions. Ministry is not exclusively for professionals or something that requires vocational time. In fact, ministry is not even optional. It's mandated. Ministry is how every faithful Christian man carries out his life—which means the entirety of life is our ministry, regardless of our vocation.

Consider Paul, who authored much of the New Testament. Here are his credentials:

> Though I myself have reason for confidence in the flesh also. If anyone else thinks he has reason for confidence in the flesh, I have more: circumcised on the eighth day, of the people of Israel, of the tribe of Benjamin, a Hebrew of Hebrews; as to the law, a Pharisee; as to zeal, a persecutor of the church; as to righteousness under the law, blameless. (Phil. 3:4–6)

Paul had tremendous real-world experience, even more than what he mentioned here. God used Paul's training, background, education, legal experience, influence, heritage, political influence, and writing and speaking abilities to transform Paul into a worldwide force for ministry in the most powerful empire of his day—the Roman Empire.

Paul is an interesting example of those men who come to Christ later in life after most of their talents, abilities, and gifts have been discovered and polished. Notice that Paul continued to use the same talents, abilities, and gifts that he'd always had. However, following Paul's conversion, God repurposed them for kingdom influence.

The book of Romans in the New Testament is one of the results. This letter, written by Paul, gives evidence of his legal skill, leadership influence, political savvy, religious upbringing, and even his knowledge of Greek and Roman philosophies. It's one of the all-time greatest legal arguments for the faith. To write it, the Lord called upon all of Paul's skills and training. From this, we can see that God had a plan for Paul and that his talents, abilities, and gifts had been repurposed for influence in a new way.

Paul understood that it was only by God's mercy and grace that this was possible:

> I thank him who has given me strength, Christ Jesus our Lord, because he judged me faithful, appointing me to his service, though

> formerly I was a blasphemer, persecutor, and insolent opponent. But
> I received mercy because I had acted ignorantly in unbelief, and the
> grace of our Lord overflowed for me with the faith and love that are
> in Christ Jesus. (1 Tim. 1:12–14)

I cannot think of a man more initially disqualified—and then, post-conversion, more perfectly qualified and repurposed—than Paul.

He's just like you, me, and every other man. As a result of God's mercy and grace, Paul was a man repurposed. Those natural talents, abilities, and gifts were leveraged for kingdom use. Formerly, Paul had used them for his purposes and glory, but now they were being used for God's purposes and glory.

God knew exactly what he would do with Paul even before his conversion. But other people weren't so sure about this "new Paul." Listen to Ananias's concern about the nature of this man's power and vendetta against believers:

> Ananias answered, "Lord, I have heard from many about this man,
> how much evil he has done to your saints at Jerusalem. And here
> he has authority from the chief priests to bind all who call on your
> name." But the Lord said to him, "Go, for he is a chosen instrument
> of mine to carry my name before the Gentiles and kings and the
> children of Israel. For I will show him how much he must suffer for
> the sake of my name." (Acts 9:13–16)

Regardless of what you see or how you feel, God is in the business of repurposing men. He is changing their vocations and altering their purposes all the time so that their intended design is aligned with his will. We, like Paul and Ananias, may not see the full picture now. But this is not our concern. Our concern is to trust God and take the next steps of obedience, and he will reveal our ministry one step at a time.

How do we do this? Let's get practical.

REFLECTION AND DISCUSSION QUESTIONS

1. Reflect on the concept that ministry is not limited to professionals or reserved for a specific stage in life but is instead a way of life for all believers. How does this perspective challenge traditional notions of ministry? Share examples of how you currently integrate your faith into your daily life and how you could further expand your ministry into your everyday interactions and activities.

2. Consider the idea of being repurposed by God for kingdom influence as exemplified by the life of the apostle Paul. Reflect on any talents, abilities, or gifts that you possess and how they could be leveraged for kingdom purposes. How can you actively seek God's guidance and surrender to his will in repurposing your skills and resources for his glory? Discuss any fears or hesitations you may have about stepping into a repurposed ministry and how you can overcome them with faith and obedience.

MINISTRY UNCOMPLICATED

To engage in our ministry and discover our gifts, there are two simple steps to take.

ONE | SMALL ACTS OF DAILY OBEDIENCE

"Teacher, which is the great commandment in the Law?" And he said to him, "You shall love the Lord your God with all your heart and with all your soul and with all your mind. This is the great and first commandment." (Matt. 22:36–38)

Imagine that scene: a curious man asks Jesus a simple question, and Jesus responds with trademark clarity. It's so simple, yet so profound.

Sometimes, we get caught up searching for what we consider Jesus's "advanced" or "deep" teachings. But in doing so, we might overlook the sheer brilliance of his straightforward wisdom. The truth is, the real depth often lies in letting his simple truths sink deeply into our hearts and minds, illuminating our motivations and transforming our lives.

That's the beauty of the teaching Jesus offers here: it's both simple and deep. Loving God wholeheartedly isn't just a commandment—it's the cornerstone of a life lived in alignment with God's will. That's why this commandment is the greatest of them all.

Here's what I mean.

I may understand that God wants me to love him with all my heart, soul, and mind, but it will take a lifetime to discover what this really means. Initially, I may believe I love him completely, only to discover after numerous daily failures that there are many places in my life where I continue to resist his love. Over time, I discover that I have not yet loved him with all my heart, soul, and mind because I love other things over him. I must let him love me more fully every day so that I can, in turn, love him—and others—more fully.

But that's what Jesus does: he makes everything simple, even our call to a life of ministry. Here is how he extends that invitation:

> While walking by the Sea of Galilee, he saw two brothers, Simon (who is called Peter) and Andrew his brother, casting a net into the sea, for they were fishermen. And he said to them, "Follow me, and I will make you fishers of men." Immediately they left their nets and followed him. (Matt. 4:18-20)

What men overcomplicate, Jesus makes simple. "Come, follow me." That's ministry. That is where a life of ministry, good works, and service begins. Jesus calls, and we go.

Most men think we are looking for a calling in the occupational sense: some specialized, ongoing task we can do for God. This is not a calling at all. Remember, Jesus is the one doing the calling. It's a *following* we seek. We are called to follow the One who is doing the leading.

As we follow, we become more like Christ. Daily in the obeying, we learn how to love him more, with all our heart, soul, and mind. We steadily subject ourselves to regular repurposing. This repurposing, initiated by Christ and empowered by the Holy Spirit, works to put to death the ways of the flesh and awaken godly motivation. It is out of this power that we do daily ministry, good works, and acts of service.

> Whatever you do, in word or deed, do everything in the name of the Lord Jesus, giving thanks to God the Father through him. (Col. 3:17)

Let's be clear: Ministry isn't just another job or even a career change. It's the essence of everything we do by the Spirit throughout our day. Every word spoken and action taken should flow from our relationship with God and contribute to his purpose. In fact, every word and action *does* flow from the condition of our relationship with God, whether we mean it to or not. That's why it's so vital to walk closely with the Lord.

> What men overcomplicate, Jesus makes simple. "Come, follow me."

At its core, ministry is an action and an outflow, not a job title. Just because some people are paid and hold leadership positions in the church doesn't mean they're the only ones called to ministry. God's idea of ministry is broader and far more inviting. He expects all believers to join in the work of ministry because we are all ministers.

As God's man, fixate less on titles and figuring out your calling, and focus more on being obedient. Follow God's call one act of obedience at a time. Titles may or may not come. Themes of ministry will reveal themselves. Through obedience, you'll discover passions and gifts to advance God's ministry and your purpose.

Let me make ministry even simpler with one question: How does God want you to follow him in obedience today? (Write out an answer right now.)

Now that you know one act of obedience, do it. This is your ministry. Commit to doing this today and every day this week. The repetition of this act of ministry for a week will encourage you to see the dynamic nature of it. As you are obedient in this way of following God, you'll discover how he is forging and defining your purpose and calling. Within a short period of time, you will be able to look back, amazed at the ministry God has been accomplishing through you.

 ## TWO | SMALL ACTS OF DAILY INFLUENCE

My beloved brothers, be steadfast, immovable, always abounding in the work of the Lord, knowing that in the Lord your labor is not in vain. (1 Cor. 15:58)

We underestimate our influence. When we act with integrity and consistency over a long period of time, our lives can have an extraordinary impact. By standing firm, being immovable in our faith, and remaining dedicated to the work of the Lord, we will inspire the people around us to change their own behavior. Integrity is hard work, but its effects multiply beyond our expectations.

We often overlook our daily influence, giving heed instead to the allure of quick fixes and shortcuts to success. As men, we sometimes even glorify this behavior when we see others using it effectively; for instance, admiring colleagues who manipulate, applauding athletes who cheat to win, or idolizing celebrities who exploit their influence for personal gain. Yet the long-term power of daily influence has compounded results. Just ask anyone in finance about the power of compound interest. One thing done regularly over a long period of time can have incredible results and produce enormous impact.

Listen to Paul's words to the Roman believers:

> God is my witness, whom I serve with my spirit in the gospel of his Son, that without ceasing I mention you always in my prayers, asking that somehow by God's will I may now at last succeed in coming to you. For I long to see you, that I may impart to you some spiritual gift to strengthen you—that is, that we may be mutually encouraged by each other's faith, both yours and mine. I do not want you to be unaware, brothers, that I have often intended to come to you (but thus far have been prevented), in order that I may reap some harvest among you as well as among the rest of the Gentiles. I am under obligation both to Greeks and to barbarians, both to the wise and to the foolish. So I am eager to preach the gospel to you also who are in Rome.
>
> For I am not ashamed of the gospel, for it is the power of God for salvation to everyone who believes, to the Jew first and also to the Greek. (Rom. 1:9–16)

I love what Paul did here. It might not seem obvious at first, but he was explaining his ministry as obedience to Christ. He also interjected his desire for an ongoing relationship with the Roman believers. In a heartfelt way, he was referencing his ministry and explaining how badly he wanted to engage in it with them. Here's the breakdown of the passage; it's simple.

» Preaching.
» Praying.

» Planning.

» Prevented—for now.

» But I'll keep on preaching, praying, and planning shamelessly anyway.

For Paul, this list was easy to recite. It wasn't rocket science. In fact, we might even say he was being overly simplistic. It wasn't a title or notoriety he sought with the believers in Rome. He desired to demonstrate obedience and to engage in small steps of hopeful, active influence over a long period of time. He stayed with it until God opened the next door, and then the next, and the next.

Because he was unable to be with this congregation in person, he persisted. He extended his ministry influence by writing a long letter to them that we know as the book of Romans—a theological masterpiece and one of the most influential books of the Bible. His letter not only reached the people of Rome, but it also reaches us today.

By remaining dedicated to the work of the Lord, we will inspire the people around us to change.

I am sure Paul had no idea that this momentary prevention of influence was going to result in even greater influence for the kingdom. Paul's wish was to preach to them in person, but God knew that a written letter would have far greater influence over time. While Paul could have worried that God's plan might be thwarted, God led him down an even more influential path, not only for Rome, but also for all believers on planet Earth. But Paul had to take that next small step of obedience in lieu of the one that had been prevented.

Sometimes, it's the small steps that matter most. Paul was a master of understanding this type of influence: one small step of obedience daily. He maintained influence by taking a small step shown by the Spirit in place of the steps he had wanted to take.

As a man of God, you need to recognize the opportunity you have to influence the people around you. You already have several circles of influence: home, work, neighbors, and friends. These are the people within your reach every day. God has placed you inside these circles, so you need to minister to them in obedience with the influence you have. Frequently, we over-look them, but we should not. They are our first ministry. Listen to this ancient command:

> Hear, O Israel: The LORD our God, the LORD is one. You shall love the LORD your God with all your heart and with all your soul and with all your might. And these words that I command you today shall be on your heart. You shall teach them diligently to your children, and shall talk of them when you sit in your house, and when you walk by the way, and when you lie down, and when you rise. You shall bind them as a sign on your hand, and they shall be as frontlets between your eyes. You shall write them on the doorposts of your house and on your gates. (Deut. 6:4-9)

These words stand tall among the Old Testament scriptures. God knows that a man who is obedient first to God and who leverages that obedience to influence those around him will, over time, be the vessel of change for himself, his home, his family, his nation, and his culture. So much potential lies within a single man who aligns himself with God, acts in obedience, and influences others along the way. As this text commands, think first of the ones you talk, sit, walk, lie, and get up with at home. Here is where your influence will be felt first.

I know this doesn't apply to every man, but some of us occasionally forget that we have a wife to lead, children to disciple, employees to guide, and neighbors to serve. Whatever our life situation, our influence always starts with those we walk most closely with. Ministry begins by living in godly obedience in ways they can observe. We must influence them in small, daily steps over a long period of time. Remember, your ministry will not take shape overnight, but it won't take shape at all unless you do the daily work required.

REFLECTION AND DISCUSSION QUESTIONS

1. Reflect on the concept of ministry as encompassing small acts of daily obedience. How does Jesus's command to love God with all our hearts, souls, and minds simplify our understanding of ministry? Share a specific example from your life where you have experienced the challenge of fully loving God in daily obedience. How can you deepen your commitment to obedience and love for God in your everyday actions?

2. Consider the power of daily influence in ministry as exemplified by Paul's approach in Romans and the instructions from Deuteronomy. Reflect on the various circles of influence in your life, such as home, work, neighbors, and friends. How can you leverage your obedience to God and your influence in these circles to advance his kingdom? Discuss any obstacles or opportunities you anticipate in applying this principle of daily influence to your ministry.

PUT IT TOGETHER

So now, to give ministry the necessary punch, we need to put these two steps together.

Obedience + Influence = Maximum Ministry Impact

Living obediently means we should naturally exert our influence. Let's say our goal is to speak more kindly to our family. This small act, when done consistently, can have a significant impact on those around us. But its influence shouldn't be underestimated. If we're genuinely convicted about the impact of our words, we might decide to take further action, like holding a family meeting after dinner.

Picture this: I turn to my wife and children at dinner and say something like: "I have come to realize that, lately, I have been coming home stressed out by the challenges at work and have been taking some of this out on each of you. First, I want you each to know I am sorry, and second, I am going to work to speak more kindly to each of you."

This statement communicates my spiritual conviction and models obedience to God. Most of the time, we think about these things privately, but sometimes, we must go public. By publicly addressing our mistakes, we make obedience visible. We don't do it to put on a show but rather to demonstrate humility and so that others can help hold us accountable. This is humble leadership.

But taking it one step further, we could appropriately leverage this to influence others. I could additionally state, "I have also noticed that this has affected how you guys speak to one another. I am not happy about how my behavior has affected you. We need to find better ways to interact with one another. So, I want you to join me in speaking more kindly to each other. Let's focus on being positive and uplifting and using a more positive tone in the house."

Now that's influence. This moment has the potential to change a family forever. Your wife and kids will never forget it. First, it is honest and self-revealing about your desire to be more obedient. Second, you used that moment to influence them toward an honoring way of life. Now picture a lifetime of moments like this with your family. Can you imagine engaging in a more powerful ministry? This is the teaching of Deuteronomy 6, and it is the result of the equation: Obedience + Influence = Maximum Ministry Impact.

Now, repeat the same process at work, with friends, and with neighbors as God allows. Here's how it could look to do this with your employee:

> "Hey, John. Yesterday at work, I came down kind of hard on you. I just wanted to tell you I reflected on how I handled that, and this morning I felt convicted, and I want to apologize. Just know I am working on this, and I want to find better ways to interact."

To your coach:

> "Coach, at practice yesterday, I felt like I handled things poorly. I was thinking and praying about it this morning, and I would like to help build a different spirit on our team. Is there something I can do?"

To your friend:

> "Steve, I noticed yesterday you were having a hard day. I was too, and I said some harsh things. I am sorry for that. Is there something I can pray about for you today?"

This is ministry—a ministry that only you can do. When you follow Jesus, you are by nature an extension of his influence, yet we take it for granted all the time. We should not hesitate to act on it, and to act on it frequently.

We also need to remember to do the actions that follow. Maximum ministry impact comes from obedience plus influence. How we obey and the spiritual application we make while obeying determine how much influence we exert. So, as I speak more kindly to everyone in my household, the manner I do it and the spiritual application I make are how I influence my family for the kingdom. It has the power to change us and others around us—forever.

Your obedience will result in influence that will leave a maximum ministry impact on others.

Never underestimate the ministry influence you wield. Start viewing your world through a spiritual lens. You're not just a plumber, builder, construction worker, designer, leader, consultant, speaker, writer, student, composer, adviser, or administrator. You're primarily a minister of the gospel. Behind each of these titles and roles lies a redeemed man with a spiritual identity.

> Maximum ministry impact comes from obedience plus influence.

Your identity holds far more weight than any earthly title you may bear. Your identity shapes all of you. You are a servant of the Highest God, a title greater than the sum of all these roles combined. Everything else comes second—even that occupation you so highly esteem. While today you might be plumbing, building, constructing, designing, leading, consulting, speaking, writing, studying, composing, advising, or administrating, your primary identity remains unchanged.

Perhaps this is why so many New Testament writers emphasized their titles this way:

Paul, a servant of Christ Jesus (Rom. 1:1)

Simon Peter, a servant and apostle of Jesus Christ (2 Pet. 1:1)

James, a servant of God and of the Lord Jesus Christ. (James 1:1)

Jude, a servant of Jesus Christ (Jude 1)

His servant John (Rev. 1:1)

We need to come to terms with our big ideas about ministry. Because guess what? Big ideas can become big idols. Even though God can redeem the profane for his purposes, men can spoil what ought to be sacred. I confess that there are times when I have aspired to have a bigger influence during my lifetime, but big ministry can be motivated by selfish intent. Ministry is something God does through all of us, not just certain ones of us. When ministry becomes a stage for our fame, it's no longer advancing God's plan for redemption.

We all have a ministry. We must carry it out via small acts over a long period of time. We plant and work and till the soil, and God is responsible for the results. If he brings about impressive outcomes, he's the one who did it, so he gets to keep all the glory. Don't become mesmerized with some big ministry out there and overlook the power of your daily influence.

Try this: Consider how God might want to use you to affect your circles of influence today. Consider the four circles of home, work, neighbors, and friends. Name the people within your circles of influence whom you need to serve in active obedience. Then act. Influence them through your obedience. Repeat that tomorrow, and then the next day, and so on.

> I long to see you, that I may impart to you some spiritual gift to strengthen you—that is, that we may be mutually encouraged by each other's faith, both yours and mine. (Rom. 1:11–12)

Let's return to the forge. Imagine the blacksmith diligently shaping a piece of metal. With each strike of the hammer, he not only conforms the metal to his will but also strengthens it. In the same way, when we live obediently to God's commands, we are like metal being shaped by the Master Blacksmith's hands. Just as the metal becomes stronger under the Blacksmith's influence, our obedience to his will strengthens our character and resolve.

And over time, his craftsmanship yields a beautiful creation. Your continued obedience and influence can shape lives for the better. Your words and actions, infused with spiritual conviction, have the power to transform hearts and minds, leaving a lasting impact on those around you. And with this, it's time to wield the sword of your obedience and influence and experience the ministry—the life—God has formed you for.

REFLECTION AND DISCUSSION QUESTIONS

1. Reflect on the equation presented: Obedience + Influence = Maximum Ministry Impact. How does this reshape your understanding of ministry? Share a personal experience where you have witnessed the combined power of obedience and influence. How can you intentionally cultivate obedience and influence in your daily interactions to maximize your ministry impact?

2. Consider the concept of humility in leadership as demonstrated through public confession and exhortation. How does humility enhance our ability to influence others for the kingdom of God? Reflect on a time when you have witnessed the transformative power of humility in leadership. How can you incorporate humility into your own leadership style to foster greater ministry impact in your circles of influence?

BUILD A
MOVEMENT

What if you and I could start a movement of men? Imagine a groundswell rising and sweeping the nation, even the world, as men respond to Jesus's call. Imagine a new season when Christian men are marked not by apathy but by obedient action.

I meet men with this type of passion all the time. They long to start a movement in their church and their community, and far beyond. Thousands of these mini-movements of men are happening all over the world. Some focus on adventure, some on retreats, some on conferences, and some on discipleship. Whatever their focus, each has begun to take up the mission and call men to act.

It's fantastic that most of these mini-movements are small. Brother, we are a small part of a sprawling and beautifully disorganized movement. Don't fail to see the ingenuity in this.

Throughout history, the task of preparing men to hear and act has been accomplished through one-on-one relationships or small groups of men. Perhaps you've been a part of a mentoring group, leadership group, or discipleship group. Within these simple one-on-one relationships, triads, or small groups, we can change the world. Yes, ourselves, our homes, our country, and our world.

Our seemingly insignificant gatherings are frequently overlooked because we do not have the flair of a big, thriving, engaging, and attractive men's ministry. But small, intimate groups could be the best choice for building a worldwide movement. This method has been tested, and guess what? It works.

Here's the evidence.

Two thousand years ago, Jesus gathered twelve previously unnoticed men: Thomas, Simon the Zealot, Philip, Simon Peter, Matthew, Jude, Judas Iscariot, John, James the son of Alpheus, James the son of Zebedee, Bartholomew, and Andrew. These men were called at different times and had a variety of life experiences and professional skills.

Jesus invested a mere two to three years into these men from the moment he called the first one until his death on the cross. During this time, this small group of men learned how to follow and live in obedience. In fact, you are reading this book today because of what Jesus invested into these twelve men two thousand years ago. Through the repetition of regular activities, Jesus developed men whom he called to act.

There's no doubt that noteworthy things can happen in massive gatherings and in large events, but the effective transmission of the gospel and manhood does not.

Are you ready to build a movement of men?

BUILD YOUR MOVEMENT

Don't overcomplicate this. Movements begin small, so start with a group of a few men and do these three things. Don't add to or subtract from these three imperatives. They work. I have used them for thirty years, and they have never failed me.

FIRST | SELECT MEN

Start by selecting some men, just like Jesus did when he chose his twelve. These were men he believed would benefit the movement in various ways. He didn't advertise on social media or put announcements in a church bulletin. He personally reached out to those he wanted. Building a movement doesn't require elaborate plans or infrastructure. It begins with you inviting one man, then another, and another.

You get what you select, so pick men from the age-group, demographic, and maturity level you are after and who face the challenges you aim to address. Look for men who are "spiritu-ally hungry"—men who connect with the call to "Come, follow me." These are the ones who are hungry and ready. They are:

> » Faithful
> » Available
> » Teachable

I call these men "FAT men." That's why they are hungry. Be proactive in selecting them. Don't wait for them to come to you. Follow Jesus's example and actively seek out the ones you want. Invite them to join you. Men love to be invited to a challenge.

Take a moment right now to jot down the names of one to twelve hungry men you would select:

SECOND | SELECT A MEETING TIME AND LOCATION

The second step in starting a movement is determining your meeting time and location. This is not brain surgery, but it's a critical step that many men don't consider.

Select a time and place that work for you, and then invite the other men to it. Tell them where you are going to be and when you will be there, and they will come if they can. If you waffle on this one, the men you've invited may begin to suspect that you are not organized and prepared. Your presence as a leader and organizer is critical, so make sure that whatever schedule you set will work for you most of the time.

By nature, you'll want to accommodate them, but when we overaccommodate, men smell weakness, and they will not follow. Jesus was strong, not soft, on this. "Come, follow me" indicates a departure from doing life as it has been. You are meeting with Jesus on his terms and his time. So why do it differently than he did?

Now write it down. When and where will you meet?

THIRD | SELECT MATERIAL

One thing that might seem complicated is the question: *What should we study or talk about when we get together?* I understand why men feel this way. There are all kinds of studies on the market today. We're swimming in an ocean of content. Combine this with the fact that men come from a variety of backgrounds, with a variety of issues and levels of spiritual maturity.

I've got an idea! Let's ditch the curriculum altogether and just use the Bible. Let's build five fundamentals into men: prayer, Scripture, brotherhood, accountability, and ministry. Then let's practice these fundamentals repeatedly and watch what God does. After all, this was Jesus's model of spiritual leadership.

We need to think more simply about this. We don't need more material than the Bible. We don't need a complicated scope and sequence for spiritual development. Men just need to hear and act, so let's support that process.

Structure a small group around the five fundamentals covered in this book. If you need an outline, try this one:

> **PRAYER** (five minutes): As a group, ask for prayer requests, and then, using the PACT method, pray.
> **SCRIPTURE** (twenty minutes): As a group, select a paragraph or section of Scripture and study it using the PASS method.

BROTHERHOOD (fifteen minutes): In pairs, use the 411 of Brotherhood method to have a discussion.

ACCOUNTABILITY (ten minutes): In pairs, practice DO accountability.

MINISTRY (ten minutes): As a group, talk about one man's ministry talents, abilities, and gifts, and learn how he used them over the last week.

ARE YOU ALL IN?

My friend, I am looking for men to lead groups just like these. It doesn't matter if your group has one man, twelve men, or a hundred men. By answering God's call and acting alongside just one other believer, you become part of the largest, most widespread movement in the world.

Our culture tends to overlook our men's groups, but who cares? We are men led by God, instructed by Christ, and guided by the Holy Spirit. Do not underestimate the power of your small, decentralized group within the movement. You may be few, but that doesn't change the impact God can have through your actions. You are God's men on God's mission for God's glory anyway. Remember, the Lord's power is unleashed by faithful action, not your personal follower count. Join the movement.

> Whatever you do, in word or deed, do everything in the name of the Lord Jesus, giving thanks to God the Father through him. (Col. 3:17)

If you are leading a group of men, I would love to hear about your adventures. Or if you need help, you can call, text, or email anytime:

Vince Miller | 651-274-8796
vince@beresolute.org | www.beresolute.org

NOTES

1. Michael Lipka, "Five Facts about Prayer," Pew Research, May 4, 2016, www.pewresearch.org/short-reads /2016/05/04/5-facts-about-prayer/.

2. Alyssa Oursler, "Is Your Gym Membership a Good Investment?," *USA Today*, April 27, 2016, www.usatoday .com/story/money/personalfinance/2016/04/27/your-gym-membership-good-investment/82758866/.

3. Larry V. Brown, s.v. "confession," *Lexham Bible Dictionary* (Bellingham, WA: Lexham Press, 2016).

4. Bob Smietana, "Americans Are Fond of the Bible, Don't Actually Read It," Lifeway Research, April 25, 2017, https://research.lifeway.com/2017/04/25/lifeway-research-americans-are-fond-of-the-bible-dont-actually-read-it/.

5. Merriam-Webster, "We Added 690 New Words to the Dictionary for September 2023," September 1, 2023, www.merriam-webster.com/wordplay/new-words-in-the-dictionary#:~:text=Signs%20of%20a%20healthy%20 language,being%20given%20to%20existing%20words.

6. Bill Mounce, "Literal Translations and Paraphrases," BillMounce.com, August 15, 2019, www.billmounce .com/monday-with-mounce/literal-translations-and-paraphrases.

7. Roy P. Basler, ed., *Collected Works of Abraham Lincoln*, vol. VII (Reply to the Loyal Colored People of Baltimore upon Presentation of a Bible, September 7, 1864), 542.

EMBRACE YOUR CALLING AS A STRONG MAN OF GOD

Available in print,
audio, and digital formats

Defining true manhood has never been more challenging. In this first book of the Forged Bible study series, popular Bible teacher Vince Miller digs deep into biblical truths to explore:

- What Jesus's life teaches us about true masculinity

- Why real strength won't be found in popular opinion

- How to discern God's design in a confusing culture

- Why the journey from sin to salvation is about Jesus, not us

- How living out authentic manhood brings purpose and joy

Designed for small group or individual use, *Essential Elements* offers the practical encouragement and answers men are looking for.

STRONG AS A MAN OF GOD

With Scripture, prayers, and actionable ideas, this devotional series from Bible teacher Vince Miller challenges you to stand up for your faith and draw closer to God. Each devotion reminds you that even in the hard moments and the stressful days, God is with you to strengthen, help, and provide.

DAVID C COOK®

JOIN US.
SPREAD THE GOSPEL.
CHANGE THE WORLD.

We believe in equipping the local church with Christ-centered resources that empower believers, even in the most challenging places on earth.

We trust that God is *always* at work, in the power of Jesus and the presence of the Holy Spirit, inviting people into relationship with Him.

We are committed to spreading the gospel throughout the world—across villages, cities, and nations. We trust that the Word of God will transform lives and communities by bringing light to the darkness.

As a global ministry with a 150-year legacy, David C Cook is dedicated to this mission. Each time you purchase a resource or donate, you're supporting a ministry—helping spread the gospel, disciple believers, and raise up leaders in some of the world's most underserved regions.

Your support fuels this mission.
Your partnership sends the gospel where it's needed most.

Discover more. Be the difference.
Visit DavidCCook.org/Donate